The Bio-psychosocial Impact of Trauma on Children and Adolescents; Suggestions for Assessment, Diagnosis and Treatment in the Jamaican Context

Jean Johnson

DEDICATION

This book is dedicated to my family and friends who supported my efforts to write this book which was first conceptualized during my research done for the PsyD and later updated to provide more recent information. I owe a depth of gratitude to the children, adolescents and their families with whom I have worked for many years and from whom I have learnt so much. This work attempts to enlighten and inspire Jamaicans living at home as well as those within the diaspora to take appropriate actions to help humanity.

TABLE OF CONTENTS

ACKNOWLEDGMENTS

I would like to acknowledge the support of several persons who assisted me with finalizing this book. Among them are Benton Allen, Patrick Mckiernan and Monica Wint.

CHAPTER 1 ~INTRODUCTION

From the beginning of history, trauma has been the common experience of humans. Some of the earliest writings contain evidence of the manifestation of psychological symptoms related to distressing experiences. Jamaica, West Indies has shared part of this common experience from the time of the Tainos around 1000 AD (http://www.indigenous portal.com), through the occupation and domination of early colonizers, the Spanish and the English. The Spaniards arrived in 1492 and enslaved the Tainos, many of whom succumbed to the harsh working conditions accompanied by a lack of immunity to European diseases such as small-pox. Others poisoned themselves instead of continuing under oppressive working requirements which were imposed on them. By 1598, less than half of the Taino population remained (http://www.indigenousportal.com). In terms of economic activities, the Spanish colony of Jamaica relied on the trading of hides and fruits with passing ships from other territories. The colonists were also involved in ship building and repairs. However, Jamaica never prospered as a Spanish colony.

During the English occupation of Jamaica from 1494 to 1655, sugar-cane came to be an important economic crop. With the decline of the numbers of native Tainos came the advent of slavery when Africans were brought to the island to work on sugar plantations as slaves. The Africans were punished harshly by being flogged and tortured for any offenses they committed. After emancipation of slavery in 1838, Jamaica's plantation owners looked for other sources of labor. East Indians and Chinese came as indentured workers for sugar plantations abandoned by some of the former slaves. These former slaves preferred to work on their own small holdings and sell their produce in the markets. From 1838 to 1917, over 30,000 East Indians immigrated to Jamaica followed by about 5,000 Chinese who arrived during 1860 to 1893. Conditions for the indentured workers were hardly better after emancipation since they too worked long hours in the hot sun, given low wages and treated inhumanely.

The first Jewish settlers arrived in Jamaica in 1530. Some of them established businesses in parts of the island while others engaged in farming. Europeans including Germans, Irish and Scottish immigrants started arriving in 1834 (Tortello, 2003). They were provided with land in various areas of the island on which they grew sugar-cane, bananas, coconuts and other crops. Today, Jamaica is a melting pot of various ethnicities although a few families have kept their pure blood lines. Why is a recounting of Jamaican history of importance to me? For me, this reflects our common heritage of sorrows mixed with joys and our failures mixed with successes.

Now we are an independent nation having gained our independence from English rule in 1962 but although we have made social and economic improvements, we are beset by various challenges that are linked to practices that can be traced to earlier periods in our history. These challenges have come at a time when new economic and social problems arise due to changes in family patterns coupled with world economic and social issues. Natural disasters namely droughts, flooding, hurricanes and storms have also wreaked havoc on our infrastructure and agricultural sector.

Historically, we have had a large number of single parent households headed mostly by females and children who are not cared for properly by their families and the state. Several children and adolescents have experienced social and economic disadvantages in this society and as a result a few agencies have been organized to provide both physical and mental health care for the young. Nevertheless, the provision of services in this country is hindered due to a shortage of funding or lack of interest by governmental authorities to provide them. As a result, there is limited material and human resources for the provision of these services.

Based on a report by the Jamaican Child Development Centre U.W.I Mona (2005), Jamaica has an extremely high rate of interpersonal violence, a problem that affects the entire population and which has been credited as the greatest single retardant to the island's development. Hickling (1994) wrote about the historical origins of aggressive attitudes and behaviors among Caribbean people resulting from the extermination of the indigenous peoples (Tianos) as well as the brutal conditions of slavery and the post-emancipation period and has suggested the utility of a historical, psychological, sociological and psychoanalytic perspective on making sense of the development of violence in the region.

Samms-Vaughn, Jackson and Ashley (2005) as well as Meeks-Gardener, Powell, Thomas and Millard (2003) state that the exposure to violence is very high in Jamaica with exposure taking on a meaning of having seen victims of homicide or knowing someone who has been murdered. There were some 1445 homicides in 2004 resulting in a rate of approximately 54 per 100,000 of the total Jamaican population which places Jamaica among the countries with the highest level of this type of crime in the world. Homicides are only the tip of the violence iceberg with vastly more people affected through injuries including maiming, medical and rehabilitation costs as well as through psychological trauma.

Research conducted by the Jamaica Child Development School of Continuing Studies UWI Mona (2005) shows that a number of interventions have been developed which aims to reduce this. However, the rates remain high and appear to be escalating for some categories of violence. Due to this problem, these researchers compiled a list of different agencies offering services to children and or adolescents from 1988 until 2005 when this report was completed. Thirty seven programs met the criteria for inclusion in this review. The services offered were psycho-educational, counseling, remedial, educational, crisis shelters, pre-vocational skill-training and small business projects.

Trauma in families is a result of frightening and sometimes violent experiences that can happen to any or all members of the family. Some types of trauma families experience are house fires, accidents, illnesses, crimes, community or school violence, sudden loss of a loved one, child abuse, domestic violence, homelessness, natural disasters and terrorism (http//wwwmdcoalition.org). Quite often the trauma affecting families also impacts children and adolescents who are members of the family. In my opinion, observational learning has an important role in influencing violence in the society. For example, Bandura's social learning theory states that aggression is learned through a process called behavior modeling. He argues that individuals do not actually inherit violent tendencies but they model them using two principles, observing aggressive models or from expecting or receiving a reward following aggression. Bandura (1977) concludes that behavior is learnt and that aggression in children is influenced by the reinforcement of family members, the media as well as the environment.

Statement of the Problem

A problem might be defined as the issue that exists in the literature, theory or practice that leads to a need to conduct a study (Creswell, 1998). There are many children and adolescents living in Jamaica who are severely traumatized and in need of assessment, correct diagnoses and the application of evidence-based treatments to help them function optimally. I hope these mental health interventions will enable individuals and their families to arrest the cycle of trauma within the Jamaican population.

Background of the Problem

This study commenced with a historical overview of the bio-psychosocial impact of various traumas experienced by generations of Jamaicans spanning over six centuries as well as the effects of some of these issues impacting our current population of children and adolescents. To achieve this goal, I have sought to review the literature on the particular disorders affecting these groups who have experienced trauma. Very limited information is available about the type of trauma experienced by many Jamaican children and adolescents and even more so about assessments and treatments of these disorders. This gap of knowledge needs to be filled so clinicians can be better prepared to help our children and adolescents cope successfully. To fill this void, I am embarking on a review of the literature available from writers/researchers based in various parts of the world relating to the topic. These studies will provide the back-drop against which further assessments, piloting and adaptation of instruments can be made. Age appropriate treatments will then be provided to ensure culture fair practices within the Jamaican context. This research project examines the bio-psychosocial impact of trauma on children and adolescents, the assessments, diagnoses and treatments of disorders resulting from trauma. It also looks at challenges in providing evidence-based treatments to these age groups. In addition, this research examines protective factors against long-term effects of trauma on children and adolescents. The knowledge gained will enable us to help young members of our population and their families to better cope with the effects of trauma. This knowledge will also help to prevent some forms of trauma that currently affect our young people.

Jamaica, like so many other countries has been faced with several challenges. These include harsh economic times, family problems, the negative impact of the media on children and adolescents as well as several other social problems. These stressors on families have contributed to broken homes, children living on the streets and to a host of different disorders manifested through truancy or other anti-social behaviors. Our island's children come from families composed of different family types. Some of these children and adolescents within these families lack adequate supervision and care. The political and social will in Jamaica has continued to leave large numbers of families including adolescents and children feeling hopeless. Some adolescents and children are abused physically or emotionally or both. Some of these abuses include sexual abuse by friends, parents, guardians or even strangers. As a result children become truants, cheat in classes, lie and become verbally and physically abusive to their class-mates, teachers and others in their homes and communities.

Despite what seems to be doom and gloom at this time, some voluntary organizations have been providing care for children and adolescents. Some of these are residential group homes while others provide recreational activities to which parents can send or take their children. Children in need of care and protection are sometimes adopted while others are placed in foster care.

Examples of residential group home facilities are the National Children's Home and Best Care Lodge. The National Children's Home focuses on children in need of care and protection due to the lack of care in families while the Best Care Lodge cares for children and adolescents with physical and mental disabilities. Children who live in and around the Kingston metropolis are provided with counseling at the Mico Counseling Center and at child guidance clinics often situated on the premises of some of the island's government-run hospitals. These hospital-based services are usually staffed with a psychiatrist and assistants.

The term complex trauma describes children's exposure to multiple or prolonged traumatic events and the impact of this exposure on their development. The National Child Traumatic Stress Network (2011) reports that typically complex trauma exposure involves the simultaneous or sequential occurrence of child maltreatment including psychological maltreatment, neglect, physical and sexual abuse as well as domestic violence. This type of trauma is chronic, begins in early childhood and occurs within the primary care-giving system. Exposure to these initial traumatic experiences and the resulting emotional dysregulation and the loss of safety, direction and the ability to detect or respond to danger cues often set off a chain of events leading to subsequent or repeated trauma exposure in adolescence and adulthood

(NCTSN, 2011). Although this definition is confined to the abuse of children within the primary care-giving system; usually the home, the occurrence of trauma can be extended to cases where they are exposed to traumatic events in communities through inter-personal violence, civil un-rest and natural disasters among other events. It is important to be able to stave-off the distressing effects impacting people especially the very young in a society. It is my belief that this is especially true in poor countries lacking the necessary resources required to care for individuals whose distress leads to physiological, behavioral and emotional abnormalities.

I have spent many years working with children and young adults even though I have had a few older persons in my educational classes, guidance and counseling sessions as well as in therapy. Due to this, I have limited my research interest to mainly the young population with which I work and intend to continue working. Based on my interests, I would like to delve further into the study of the bio-psychosocial impact of trauma on children and adolescents, the disorders which are diagnosed in those who have experienced trauma and how these disorders can be best assessed and treated using evidence-based therapies. The information gained will increase my ability to psycho-educate and render therapeutic services needed in my country and may be of benefit to other professionals as well.

Events that Cause Trauma

There has been an increasing interest in addressing the needs of children and adolescents who have become traumatized to the point where a few of them living in Jamaica have taken their own lives. It appears that despite the efforts of the Ministry of Education and health services providers, the issue is still on-going. As I write, I am listening to a news program while the host interviews a senior education officer from the Guidance and Counseling Unit at the Ministry of Education. In this interview, she reports that over one-million calls were received over a few weeks from the public to their recently organized call centers expressing concern about the high incidence of recent suicidal deaths among children.

Examples of recent incidences in Jamaica inevitably leaving several families traumatized were outlined in the Sunday Gleaner of April 24, 2011. To maintain anonymity, I have replaced the given names of the children and adolescents who died within a few weeks with pseudonyms. On April 7, 2011, sixteen year old Bobby Smith was killed by his step-father along with three adult members of his family. The class-mates of this student were traumatized and were provided with group counseling by the Ministry of Education. Then on April 12, 2011, twelve year old Samantha Dawes was killed by an adult family member along with two older members of her family.

Several suicides involving children and adolescents occurred since the start of 2011, commencing with Moya Brown who hung herself in Western Jamaica on March 30, 2011 and 14 year old Georgia Dennis who on the 8th of April also hung herself for unknown reasons. The third suicide occurred on April 10, 2011 when 14 year-old Terena Young hung herself after an argument with her mother. Yet another suicide occurred when Martin Whyte, eight years old hung himself during the first week of June 2011 followed shortly after by 18 year-old Peaches Jones who left a letter outlining her reasons for taking her own life.

Two other news items during August and September 2011 highlighted murders committed by female adolescents who took the lives of their younger male siblings. These and other incidences have led concerned persons in this society to seek answers as to why children and youths have been taking their own lives as well as others.

There are weekly reports about school violence in several schools throughout the island. These include stabbings resulting in life-threatening injuries and even deaths. Not only are adolescents attacking their peers in schools but recently there are increasing reports about students attacking teachers.

In addition, children experience trauma as a result of a number of different circumstances such as sexual, physical and emotional abuse. For example, during September 2012 there was public outcry about the recent trend of males sexually assaulting children and adolescents in several communities throughout Jamaica.

Other traumatic events can be attributed to exposure to domestic violence, severe natural disasters such as floods, fires, earthquakes, community violence or military actions that result in trauma. Other factors resulting in trauma for youngsters are abandonment, witnessing violence in the neighborhood or school setting including fights, drive-by shootings and law enforcement actions. Personal attacks by a person or an animal, kidnapping or bullying may also result in trauma. In addition, medical procedure(s) including surgery, accidents or serious illnesses can result in trauma as well. Hence traumatic events impacting young members of this society have been recurrent and horrific.

Mass trauma is defined by Weiling and Mittal (2008) as crises ranging from hurricanes and earthquakes to civil war, genocides and famine. In view of these events and their impact on different populations, these authors recommend that interventions should simultaneously consider:

The diverse historical, socio-political, economic, racial/ethnic, gender and cultural factors that often contribute to events like war and organized violence impacting the course and type of social and psychological responsibilities given to the occurrences of natural disasters within the world. The broad and multiple dimensions of mass trauma sometimes vary enormously in the etiology, symptomology and phenomenological meaning given and the eco-systemic levels of the targeted intervention.

Even though there are many cases of untreated trauma, in one report found at http://www.pioj.gov.jm, it was noted that after the West Kingston violence in May 2010, special exercises including individual therapy and group counseling were provided for the young who were traumatized by the sound of gunshots and the deaths of persons within their community.

Meanwhile, Dr. Wright a psychiatrist employed by the Jamaican Government, highlighted the paucity of skilled mental health professionals hired in the public sector. He reported that only four clinical psychologists were hired by the Jamaican government and only a few mental health clinics were staffed with any of these professionals. This information can be understood against the size of the population of this island which is estimated to be 2,909,714 as of June 2013. With regards to access to treatment in 2006, Dr. Wright explained that children and adolescents were treated for various disorders including depression and mood disorders with pharmacological interventions in a twenty-bed psychiatric ward at the University Hospital. He noted that these children usually share the ward with older psychiatric patients. http://www.who.int/mental_health/Jamaica_who

Purpose of the Study
The purpose of this study is to investigate the bio-psychosocial impact of trauma on children and adolescents and to seek available information about assessments, diagnoses and treatments of disorders within this population. I have reviewed the literature on the status of mental health services provided in Jamaica for the youthful population when compared to diagnostic and treatment options available for this group internationally. In addition, I have had conversations with colleagues to gain insights about their present practices to provide information on how these disorders can be best assessed, diagnosed and treated using evidence-based therapies in Jamaica.

Theoretical Framework
The current review of the literature is important within the Jamaican context, since I am unable to establish conclusively the extent of the impact of trauma on children and adolescents in this country as well as the assessment, diagnostic and treatment practices in which mental health professionals are engaged. There is limited available research on the disorders occurring in children and adolescents in this country.

However, I have found a few studies that discuss the impact of violence on these groups and some means of assessment used to identify disorders in this population in Jamaica but only a few efficacious treatments are mentioned in the literature.

Nevertheless, the literature review examining the bio-psychosocial impact of trauma on children and adolescents as well as the assessment, diagnosis and treatment of some disorders mainly post-traumatic stress disorder (PTSD) and complex post-traumatic stress disorder (CPTD) is extensive. Evidence based treatments originating from theorists like Aaron Beck's (1976) work on cognitive theory is a fore-runner for cognitive behavior therapy (CBT), laying the foundation for trauma focused cognitive behavior therapy (TFCBT) used for treating children and younger adolescents.

Research questions
The following questions will guide this research:

What is the bio-psychosocial impact of trauma on children?

What is the bio-psychosocial impact of trauma on adolescents?

How can disorders that result from trauma be best assessed, diagnosed and treated in children?

How can disorders that result from trauma be best assessed, diagnosed and treated in adolescents?

What are some challenges providing evidence-based treatments to children and adolescents?

What are some protective factors against long-term effects of trauma on children and adolescents?

Importance of the Study
Jamaica is one of the islands located in the Northern Caribbean area. On these islands including Jamaica, a physician is generally the first point of entry for patients seeking help with many receiving psychotherapy (Johnson, Weller, Williams-Brown and Pottinger, 2008). There is a prevailing belief in the Jamaican culture that people should solve their own problems and not involve others. In these relationships the patient expects to be passive while the doctor decides and informs him/her what should be done. This belief and practice continues in the psychotherapeutic relationship when the client expects the psychologist to inform him/her of what is happening because it is his responsibility to do so. These authors note that this expectation for a quick solution may prevent their perseverance and hinder them from developing a relationship and obtaining relief of symptoms.

The search for an answer regarding the use and efficacy of any treatment(s) used in the therapy of traumatized children and adolescents in Jamaica has proved inconclusive, although Johnson and Coley (2008) report that an informed survey of Caribbean psychotherapists and counselors reveal many practitioners generally use an eclectic approach in treating patients seeking psychological relief. In interviewing a few colleagues who work in counseling centers here, I learnt that the Gestalt-type therapy was mainly used in addressing concerns of adolescents. Some also used bibliotherapy which they disclosed can lead the client to identify themselves with a character, event and ideas presented in a story. This allowed youngsters to discuss and examine issues and to seek solutions to their problems. A few others used play-therapy to assist young children in regulating their emotions.

Summary and Organization of the Remaining Chapters

In chapter one I presented a brief synopsis of the historical and socio-economic factors impacting our Jamaican people over the centuries. Traumatic events have been inherent within this culture for centuries and the likely impact this would have had on the psyche of our people would have been tremendous. This trend is not abating as new challenges are now presented with which Jamaicans have to cope. In seeking to address these needs, chapter two provides answers to six questions relating to the bio-psychosocial impact of trauma on children and adolescents (0–21 years) in Jamaica and other countries. The disorders diagnosed in those who have been impacted, assessed and received evidence-based treatments could likely be adapted for use within our population. Chapter three provides a thorough analysis of the key findings and a summary of them. This final chapter will examine conclusions drawn from the findings, examine the meanings and implications of the study along with a call for action to deal with our young as well as make recommendations for future research.

CHAPTER 2 ~ REVIEW OF LITERATURE

In chapter one, I considered the circumstances that contributed to trauma throughout generations of people in the Jamaican context and some of the impact this would have had on the inhabitants of this country. My reason for saying this is that during these years, observational learning would affect the way people recognize and process trauma and faced with the expanded role of the media in our society, communication about specific traumatic incidences are highlighted daily. In view of the fore-going, I am interested in examining the impact of daily negative occurrences on the present generation of children and adolescents by reviewing the available literature on the topic as well as seeking to find what diagnoses are made after assessments, what treatments are used by clinicians as well as their reported efficacy in Jamaica.

In addition, it is my intention to examine the bio-psychosocial impact of trauma on children and adolescents in other parts of the world as well as some protective factors to stave off some of the ill effects. I will investigate how these disorders are assessed, diagnosed and treated using evidence-based therapies as well as other treatments which are viewed as probably efficacious. I would like to suggest that Jamaicans can learn from what happens elsewhere which could lead us to further investigate how any of these modes of assessment and treatment can be adapted for use within our context. One reason for examining the literature written about other countries is that the available Jamaican research providing answers to the questions is limited in scope so the findings will serve to inform readers about these matters. In view of this, I will commence with a review of the international literature and progress to what is applicable for the Caribbean/Jamaican context.

What is the bio-psychosocial impact of trauma on children?

Trauma is the experience, threat or witnessing of physical harm and the associated helplessness, fear or horror attached to that experience which is more common than sometimes believed. A traumatic event is an event which threatens injury, death of the physical body of a child or adolescent while causing shock, terror or helplessness (First, Frances, Pincus, 2002). Young (2010) confirms the findings of Briere and Lanktree (2008) that exposure to various forms of trauma appears relatively common during childhood.

Kearney, Wechsler, Kaur and Lemos-Miller (2009) outlined the Federal Child Abuse Prevention and Treatment Act of 1974 which defines youth maltreatment as any recent act or failure to act on the part of a parent or caretaker which results in death, serious physical or emotional harm, sexual abuse or exploitation or an act or failure to act which presents an imminent risk of serious harm.

These researchers provide an additional definition from the American Psychological Association Committee on professional practice and standards that defines maltreatment as "actions that are abusive, neglectful, or otherwise threatening to a child's welfare" (1988, p. 16). Dubowitz and Bennett (2007) define maltreatment in youth mainly as neglect which includes omission of care or not adequately meeting a child's basic needs.

The annual frequency of youth maltreatment practice and standards also defines maltreatment as actions that are abusive, neglectful or otherwise threatening to a child's welfare (APA, Committee on Professional Practice and Standards, 1998). Courtis (2008) notes that the expanded understanding of trauma now extends to all forms of domestic violence and attendant trauma occurring in the context of family as well as other intimate relationships. These forms of intimate domestic abuse often occur over extended time periods during which the victim is entrapped and conditioned in a variety of ways. In the case of child abuse, the victim is psychologically and physically immature and his or her development is often seriously compromised by repetitive abuse and inadequate response at the hands of family members or others on whom he or she relies for safety and protection. The expanded understanding also extends to other types of catastrophic, deleterious and entrapping traumatization occurring in childhood.

It is important to note that the bio-psychosocial impact of trauma on children relate to the strong effects of various factors on their physical, cognitive and emotional dimensions. Some events may relate to family violence which can include physical or emotional aggression and involve at least one family member as a victim and another as a perpetrator. Actions vary widely in severity from minor aggression from pushing, shoving and slapping to the death of a family member (Margolin and Vickerman, 2007). Moreover, the physical and psychological impact of specific aggressive acts varies not only by severity but also by size and developmental stage of the recipient. For instance, shaking can be fatal to a young infant but is unlikely to injure an adolescent.

Impact also takes into account disruption to the family system including family dislocation. These researchers report when there is violence in the home, it often leads to one parent leaving with the youth receiving an out-of-home placement or temporary relocation to a domestic violence shelter with their mother and siblings. Additionally, affect dysregulation in survivors of early trauma may have led them to survive through disassociation creating their inability to learn how to moderate excessive emotions or may result in problematic methods of thinking, remembering or perceiving (Ford, 2005).

It has been established that severe psychological trauma causes impairment of the neuro-endocrine systems in the body (Moroz, 2005). Extreme stress triggers the fight or flight survival response, activates the sympathetic and suppresses the parasympathetic nervous system. Fight or flight responses increases cortisol levels in the central nervous system which enables the individual to take action to survive by either dissociation, hyper-arousal or both. At extreme levels, this can cause alterations in brain development and destruction of brain cells. This loss of neurons and their connections is associated with deficiency of emotional regulation, logical thinking and social behavior seen in maltreated children (Putman, 2006).

It is believed that in children high levels of cortisol can disrupt cell differentiation, cell migration and critical aspects of central nervous system integration and functioning. Trauma affects basic regulatory processes in the brain stem, the limbic brain which regulates emotion, memory, regulation of arousal and affect, the neocortex perception of self and the world as well as integrative functioning across the central nervous system. Moroz (2005) explains that traumatic experiences are stored in the child's body/mind and as such fear, arousal and dissociation associated with the original trauma may continue after the threat of danger and arousal has subsided. Development of the capacity to regulate affect may be undermined or disrupted by trauma so children exposed to acute or chronic trauma may show symptoms of mood swings, impulsivity, emotional irritability, anger and aggression, anxiety, depression and dissociation. Early trauma particularly trauma at the hands of a caregiver can markedly alter a child's perception of self, trust in others and perception of the world. Children who experience severe early trauma often perceive that they may not live a long time since life is dangerous so they give up hope and expectations for themselves.

Rossman and Ho (2000) describe children growing up in abusive families as living in a type of war zone. They believe that sometimes children can predict the attacks and sometimes the aggression is unexpected. This leads to victims experiencing a sense of danger and uncertainty. Children's experiences of intense physical child abuse and domestic violence produce affective and physiological reactions. While severity of violence exposure is one factor affecting the development of PTSD, other factors such as accumulation of multiple stressors, functioning of the non-offending caregiver and the child's perception of the stressor also are significant variables that may influence the development of this disorder.

Gewirtz, Forgatch and Wieling (2008) explain that trauma typically presents in the context of circumstances that may influence child adjustment including type of trauma, the number of co-occuring adversities, the mental and physical health of children and caregivers, resilience factors within the family and children's developmental stages. In addition, the researchers state that all these variables can profoundly impact the quality of parenting practices following mass-trauma events which will mediate the relationship between trauma exposure, child adjustment and intervention to support parenting which have the potential to improve children's outcomes significantly.

Moroz (2005) notes that among the most devastating effects of early trauma is the disruption of the child's individuation and differentiation so as to create a separate sense of self. Fragmentation of the developing self occurs in response to stress that overwhelms the child's limited capacities for self-regulation. So survival becomes the focus of the child's interactions and activities hence adapting to the demands of their environment takes priority. Since traumatized children lose their identity in the process of coping with ongoing threats to their survival, they cannot afford to trust, relax or fully explore their own feelings, ideas or interests. Young trauma victims often come to believe there is something inherently wrong with them, that they are at fault, unlovable, helpless and unworthy of protection and love. Such feelings can lead to poor self-image, self-abandonment and self destructiveness. Ultimately these feelings may create a victim state of body, mind and spirit that leaves the individual vulnerable to subsequent trauma and re-victimization.

Kearney, et al. (2009) highlight that repetitive traumatic events such as ongoing and severe maltreatment create widespread biological and psychological ill effects in youth. They add that factors such as socioeconomic adversities, family conflict, caregiver's psychopathology or addiction contribute further to complex trauma reactions in the child. Van der Kolk, (2005) state that features of disorganized attachment is a frequent feature in families where abuse is rife. This writer notes that children who are reared in these environments have increased susceptibility to stress. For example, they have difficulty focusing their attention and modulating arousal, the inability to regulate emotions without external assistance as they experience feelings and act overwhelmed by intense or numbed emotions. They also experience altered help-seeking that is, seeking help excessively and dependency or social isolation and disengagement.

It has been established that brain development occurs mainly in childhood and adolescence. The development of disorders occurs as a result of the interaction of genetics and experiences persons have had. If there is failure or distortion of requisite experiences through abuse and victimization this may have long-term effects on brain function and even structure (Carey, 2008). This writer provides proof that poorer functioning commonly affects mood regulation, frustration-tolerance and levels of attention. Numerous brain hormones are normally released in response to stress and regulate a wide range of body functions through structures including the hypothalamus, pituitary and adrenal glands. So severe childhood stress damages the normal responsiveness of this system and this may persist into adulthood. As a result of repeated stress, the sensitivity of brain cells in some particularly vulnerable people can cause significant damage to the cells in the hippocampus. It is this damage that seemingly explains the abnormalities in brain function mentioned before.

Cicchetti and Toth, (2005) note that child maltreatment is associated with a range of impairment in areas of basic functioning (eating, sleep), cognition (attention, memory, learning, academic achievement), affective style (modulation, regulation, mood disorders), motivation and relationships. More specifically, early trauma can lead to dysregulation of the hypothalamic–pituitary–adrenal (HPA) axis. The HPA axis is responsible for releasing glucocorticoids to enhance coping with stress. Glucocorticoids that have received great attention in the area of maltreatment include cortisol and adrenocorticotropic hormone (ACTH). The HPA axis and it's glucocorticoids are especially important for responding to stressful situations involving novelty, negative emotional content and feelings of lack of control (Kearney, et al. 2009). Carpenter, Carvalho, Tyrka, Wier, Mello and Mello (2007), suggest that exposure to stress and concomitant hypothalamus-pituitary-adrenal (HPA) axis activation during early development can have deleterious effects such as mood, anxiety disorders, major depressive disorder and PTSD during adulthood. Heim and Nemeroff (2009) explain that glucocorticoids are also a key part of a negative feedback loop with the hippocampus that signals the hypothalamus to end glucocorticoid release. Further, decreased cortisol secretion over time can thus lead to sustained activation of neural and other systems involved in reactions to stress and fear. Handwerger (2009) explains that maladaptive HPA axis functioning may involve failure to activate when necessary, activation when unnecessary or failure to end glucocorticoid release when the stressor has been fully dealt with. Kearney et al. (2009) note that such dysfunction may be a key part of allostatic overload in maltreated youth.

Anda, Croft, Felliti, Nordenberg, Giles, Williamson and Giovino (1999) postulate that adverse childhood experiences (ACEs) are understood to be trauma exposures that constitute a frequent and common problem that leads to increased risk of unhealthy behaviors, risk of violence or re-victimization, disease, disability and premature mortality as people develop and age. This writer explains that neuroscientists have linked childhood maltreatment using experimental animal models as well as case-control studies in humans to long-term changes in brain structure and function, involving several inter-connected brain regions including the prefrontal cortex, hippocampus, amygdala, corpus callosum and cerebellum. Early stress is also associated with lasting alterations in stress-responsive neurobiological systems, including the hypothalamic-pituitary-adrenal axis and monoamine neurotransmitter systems. These lasting effects on the developing brain would be expected to affect numerous human functions into adulthood including emotional regulation, somatic signal processing (body sensations), substance abuse, sexuality, memory, arousal and aggression.

Kearney, et al. (2009) articulate that the HPA axis is not fully developed at birth and is thus subject to environmental experiences that shape it's activity. Most children experience a decline in HPA activity during preschool years as they learn to cope with stressors so they identify most threats as mild and receive appropriate and supportive feedback from parents. Children faced with abusive parents however may be at risk for poor regulation of the HPA axis. Secure attachment status, appropriate social/parental feedback, responsible and sensitive parental care appear to be especially important influences on appropriate HPA axis development in the early years. Given the established finding that the developing HPA system is under strong social regulation in young children it is not surprising that providing a more sensitive, responsive care-giving context would be an effective intervention for maltreated children (Tarullo and Gunnar, 2006).

Disorganized attachment following severe maltreatment from a caregiver is the pathway to social, emotional and cognitive impairments that lead to increased risk of unhealthy behaviors, risk of violence or re-victimization, disease, disability and premature mortality as people develop and age. Significant elevations in cortisol secretion during toddlerhood can occur as a result of disordered attachment occurring during this early period of their lives. Watts-English, Fortson, Gibler, Hooper and DeBellis (2006) note that school-aged children who have been physically and sexually maltreated often exhibit substantial elevations in cortisol as well. In addition increased ACTH levels have been found among adults with a history of maltreatment.

Bruce, Fisher, Pears and Levine (2009) conclude from their study that maltreated foster children showed significant alterations in their morning cortisol production compared to non-maltreated children. They state that even though low morning cortisol levels were the characteristic pattern observed in the foster children, the levels varied depending upon their maltreatment experiences. In conclusion, these results suggest that the HPA system responds differentially to specific types of early adverse experiences.

Conversely however, lower cortisol levels have been reported for neglected and severely deprived children even into adulthood (Van der Vegt, Van der Ende, Kirschbaum, Verhulst, and Tiemeier, 2009). These researchers report that after investigating the long-term relationship between reported early maltreatment and the stress-system in a large adult sample of international adoptees, it was found that neglect and abuse together with neglect early in life predicted alterations of the HPA axis even if a different environment was experienced after the early maltreatment. Notably profound maltreatment was related to lower cortisol levels that showed a steadier decline than cases of less severe early maltreatment which was associated with higher levels of cortisol and a steeper diurnal decline. These researchers suggest that the severity of the early maltreatment may be related to the basal cortisol pattern or otherwise the lowest cortisol reading achieved after sleep.

Kearney, et al. (2009) write that dysregulation of glucocorticoids over an extended period of time has been linked to anxiety and mood disorders as well as deficits in learning, memory and response inhibition. They posit that HPA axis dysregulation or dysfunction may therefore be an important conduit between early trauma such as maltreatment and subsequent psychiatric disorder. Alternatively it is possible that a child with a dysfunctional HPA system may behave inappropriately and aggressively, thereby increasing the chances of maladaptive parenting practices. Another possibility however, is that those children with HPA axis dysregulation act aggressively and otherwise inappropriately leading to maladaptive disciplinary practices (Van Voorhees and Scarpa, 2004).

Findings regarding HPA axis dysregulation and psychiatric disorder among maltreated children are not universal, however. One reason may be that onset of puberty, genetic factors, gender, current psychotic diagnosis, current life stresses and social support may influence the degree to which the HPA system is able to adapt to the current life situation versus the early maltreatment context and may help moderate cortisol levels (Tarullo and Gunnar, 2006).

Kaufman, Yang, Palumberi, Housheryar, Lipschitzn, Krystal and Geleruter (2004) and Perry (2009), explain that resilient children recover quickly from stressful experiences or isolated traumatic episodes which may not lead to widespread biological changes. In addition some children are perhaps buffered from major HPA axis dysregulation or other biological effects following maltreatment through certain genotypes, good affect regulation and cognitive functioning, positive self-concept, social support and optimal subsequent care-giving experiences. Adoption with high-quality care-giving has been found to reverse the hypothalamic pituitary axis alterations which result from stress, distress and trauma typically observed in association with early stress factors.

Watts-English, et al. (2006) state that many maltreated youth however are likely to experience HPA axis dysregulation which can relate to major brain system dysfunctions. They note that major neurobiological stress response systems namely the sympathetic nervous system (SNS), the serotonin system and the limbic-hypothalmic-pituitary-adrenal (LHPA) axis significantly influences arousal, stress reactions, physical and cognitive development. Under chronic stress the immune system may also be affected. The neurobiological stress systems are interconnected at many levels so dysregulation in one system can lead to problems in others. Memory, learning and spatial information processing may thus be affected.

Kearney, et al. (2009) posit that trauma early in life can also increase sympathetic nervous system responsiveness and affect serotonergic, noradrenergic, and dopaminergic systems. Kaufman and Charney (2001) note that changes in these systems could help explain the presence of later psychiatric disorders such as anxiety or depression although there is emerging proof that familial-genetic factors also influence the likelihood of maltreated children developing depressive disorders, in particular major depressive disorder. So all of these changes can be greatly moderated by genetic and familial influences and the quality of subsequent care-giving. Cicchetti and Toth (2005) posit that diminution in startle responses to angry faces seen by abused children may suggest that they have experienced structural brain stem abnormalities. They note further that these changes reflect significant impairments of the sympathetic and parasympathetic nervous systems as well as key neurochemical and hormonal systems, HPA axis dysregulation, structural brain changes and other biological systems which contribute to serious psychological effects. These psychological effects generally include disruption of key developmental achievements in motor, emotional, behavioral, language, social, academic and cognitive skills (DeBellis, 2005). As a consequence these widespread disruptions can produce a general inability to sufficiently integrate physical sensations, emotions and cognitions and thus lead to disorganized methods for behavioral self-regulation and coping with stress. In effect, chronically maltreated youths have great difficulty understanding their surrounding environment and may not develop or execute appropriate methods for coping with stress or solving problems. Problems in emotional and behavioral self-regulation which is a result of childhood maltreatment can then lead to excessive anxiety, depression, cognitive distortions, somatization, dissociation, aggression, impulsivity, suspiciousness and other systemic maladaptive responses (Kaplow and Widom, 2007; Putnam, 2003).

Kearney et al., (2009) in a review of contemporary research and thought provide proof that PTSD can afflict youths if they are maltreated. These researchers examine epidemiological, symptomatological, prognostic, etiological and clinical characteristics. Carrion, Weems, Watson, Eliez, Menon, and Reiss (2009) found that twenty-four children and adolescents (aged 7–14) with a history of interpersonal trauma and gender matched controls underwent structural magnetic resonance imaging. Images of the Pre Frontal Cortex (PFC) and midline brain structures were first analyzed using volumetric image analysis. The findings revealed abnormal frontal lobe morphology as seen in separate-complementary image analysis methods and reduced pons and posterior vermis areas which are associated with pediatric PTSD. Frontal lobe abnormalities in pediatric PTSD are of particular interest from the perspectives of developmental psychiatry and cognitive neuroscience. These researchers report that laboratory studies recently reported an attenuation of frontal lobe asymmetry in children with PTSD symptoms. Beers and DeBellis (2002) state that in a study of children with PTSD, results showed that they performed more poorly on measures of attention and abstract reasoning. These authors caution that they do not know if these results are related to maltreatment or the presence of an anxiety disorder.

Additionally these findings may be explained by the presence of comorbid psychiatric disorders, particularly mood disorders in the children with PTSD. This is seen as consistent with prefrontal dysfunction or executive dysfunction in their brains. Sensory experiences associated with traumatic events are closely intertwined with physiological reactions and over time with alterations in biological stress systems. DeBellis (2005) reports that repeated neural activation due to trauma exposure can alter the quantity and quality of neurotransmitter release. He reports that prolonged stress due to family violence exposure and/or sexual abuse has been linked to chemical changes in the brain such as higher levels of norepinephrine (noradrenaline), dopamine, epinephrine, adrenaline and cortisol. Elevations in adrenaline and noradrenaline prepares the body for quick action through increased heart rate and blood flow and also increases agitation and perhaps decreases attention. After prolonged exposure, the body regulates arousal by decreasing the number of receptors for arousal (Margolin and Vickerman, 2007). Also high levels of glucocorticoids are associated with damage in the hippocampus which can negatively impact memory. Schwartz and Perry (1994) speculate that the developing brain's plasticity makes it more susceptible to formation of malignant memories that affect not only the stress response system but also the emerging organizations of neural networks regulating other basic states and characteristics of the individual.

In a study by Shevlin, Dorahy and Adamson (2007) a modified version of the composite International Diagnostic Interview was used to assess the life-time prevalence of non-affective psychosis consisting of schizophrenia, schizophreniform disorder and atypical psychosis. They asked five questions representing childhood victimizations; threats to physical abuse, serious physical attacks and assaults, forced sex and sexual molestation. All analyses were conducted using hierarchical binary logistic regression in SPSS 11.0. These authors reported childhood physical abuse as the only significant predictor of psychosis in the entire sample after depression. Shevlin, et al. (2007) explained that the current findings support the notion that childhood physical abuse may be one experience that alters neurobiological development and increases the risk for a psychiatric illness. It can be noted that cumulative trauma may also operate to further heighten risk of a psychotic illness.

Chronically traumatized children tend to experience pronounced alterations in states of consciousness with amnesia, hypemnesia, dissociation, depersonalization and derealization, flashbacks and nightmares of specific events, school issues, difficulties in inattention regulation involving orientation in time and space as well as sensorimotor developmental disorders (Van der Kolk, 2005). Stirling and Amaya-Jackson (2008); Thompson, Crosby, Wonderlich, Mitchell, Redline, Demuth, Smith and Haseltine (2003); state that maltreatment is linked to a number of internalizing and externalizing behavioral problems including emotional instability, substance abuse, anxiety, depression, suicidality, an eating disorder and aggression, as well as other self destructive behaviors. Other problems include increased risk for bipolar disorder, unsafe sexual behavior, obesity, low self-esteem, criminal behavior, delayed language, cognition and low IQ (Haugaard and Hazan, 2003; Veltman and Browne, 2001).

Diehl and Prout (2002) state that a sexually abused child is more likely to compare himself less favorably with his peers and incorporate beliefs in his inferiority, hence lacking self-efficacy. Among children in families who reported for family violence, whether or not they experienced nonspecific fear, fear of injury or fear of death during violent episodes these were important predictors of PTSD among family members (Saunders, 2003). It is also believed that youngsters who do not have adequate social support are at risk of experiencing a higher level of hopelessness and behavioral problems. Kaplow and Widom (2007) note that an early onset of child abuse contributes to various psychopathologies such as depression, substance abuse, personality disorders, posttraumatic stress and other anxiety disorders in adulthood.

Bartley-Small (2010) writing about disorders of children in the Jamaican society state that there is an apparent relationship between socioeconomic status and depressive symptoms in children and adolescents between 6 to 12 years of age. She posits that children whose parents are from the higher and middle-high socioeconomic status are at lesser risk of experiencing depressive symptoms than those of low socioeconomic status, although children living in single parent households as well as families of lower socio-economic status have comparatively the same level of depressive symptoms. This writer concludes that there is a positive relationship between exposure to violence and depressive symptoms in children.

A comprehensive review of the available Jamaican/Caribbean literature reveals there are violence prevention programs in Jamaica that address bio-psychosocial issues among children and adolescents. However, there is limited research that answers my questions about the impact of trauma on children and adolescents in Jamaica. Crawford-Brown (1999) reveals that the family constellation which includes absence of mother, low contact with mother, low contact with father, instability in living arrangement and close relations with conduct-disordered peers places a child at risk for the effect and presence of conduct disorder.

What is the bio-psychosocial impact of trauma on adolescents?

Perry (2009) contends that older age of onset of maltreatment and gender may be a protective factor in preventing its ill-effects. Lemos-Miller (2008) found that trauma-related cognitions and dissociation were connected to PTSD symptoms in maltreated adolescents if a substantial amount of depression was involved. Depression in this study consisted of negative mood, interpersonal problems, ineffectiveness, anhedonia and negative self-esteem.

Maltreatment and PTSD contributes to lower self-efficacy or a belief that one is not in control of one's emotional experiences which may help to explain the frequency of depression in adolescents. Collin-Vezina and Herbert (2005) assessed dissociation and PTSD symptoms in a group of school-age girls who disclosed that they were sexually abused. The results indicated high levels of dissociation and PTSD among this group with 46% presenting with clinical levels of PTSD symptomatology and 30% with clinical levels of dissociative tendencies. In a study conducted among a non-clinical population of youths, Briere and Scott (2006) concluded that the relationship between trauma and significant dissociative symptomatology is probably moderated by a number of other variables including level of posttraumatic stress and existing affect regulation capacities of traumatized individuals. Such findings may have clinical implications according to these researchers in that they may interfere with remediation of disassociated emotions and likely relate to many of the biological and attachment problems discussed in children previously. They conclude that the relationship between trauma and significant dissociative symptomatology is probably moderated by a number of other variables including in the current study, level of posttraumatic stress and existing affect regulation capacities. They note that such findings may have clinical implications and fit an integrated model of maltreatment effects such as PTSD based on self-regulation deficits, depression and social support. Halligan, Michael, Clark and Ehlers, (2003) explain that persistent dissociation and negative interpretations of trauma memories maintain PTSD symptoms.

Kearney, et al. (2009) highlight that a psychobiological approach is a popular model for conceptualizing the effects of maltreatment. This model involves a cascading sequence of intense, aversive environmental stressors, key changes in biological systems creating poor coping and problematic self-regulation of behavior, subsequent and wide-ranging psychological problems and devastating long-term effects. This model also assumes an ecological-transactional relationship among many variables such as the interplay among biological and familial factors (Cicchetti and Toth, 2005). These researchers provide a synopsis of key research findings regarding this cascading sequence. They report that biological effects of maltreatment aside from those directly related to assault include systemic brain changes in growth, maturation, neural development and plasticity as well as indirect influences of stress, neglect and poor attachment. These changes can contribute to adverse brain development and compromised neuropsychological and psychosocial outcomes.

Mueser and Taub (2008) posit that PTSD is a common but under diagnosed disorder among adolescents with severe emotional and behavioral disorders who are involved in multiple service systems. Due to this, they recommend that routine screening for trauma exposure and PTSD be conducted with all adolescents receiving mental health services so that treatment can be provided to those with this diagnosis. However, in one study, VanderKolk, Pynoos, Cicchetti, Maylene, D'Andrea, Putman, Stolbach, Cloitre, Lieberman, Glenn, Sinzzala and Teicher, (2009) found that acute stress disorder dissociation criterion appears to have no unique role in the prediction of later PTSD in a large sample of young trauma survivors homogeneous for trauma, although intense psychological problems such as these can translate into long-term effects. Common long-term effects of maltreatment include school failure, anxiety, depression and other post-traumatic disorders, drug abuse and in later life, engaging in violence similar to that which they were originally exposed (Harris, Lieberman and Marans, 2007).

Mauser and Taub (2008) explained a traumatic event can be defined by it's capacity to provoke fear, helplessness or horror in individuals as a response to the threat of injury or death of someone. Those persons exposed to such events are at increased risk not only for post-traumatic stress disorder (PTSD) but also for major depressive disorder (MDD), panic disorder, generalized anxiety disorder (GAD) and substance abuse as well as somatic symptoms and physical illnesses, particularly hypertension, asthma and chronic pain syndromes. It is also believed that large numbers of adolescents with substance use disorders (SUDs) also have trauma histories (50%-75%), have developed PTSD (11%-47%) or both issues (Khouri, Tang, Bradley, Cabells and Ressler, 2010).

Holbrook and Hoyt (2004) enunciate that one of the most consistent findings in the epidemiology of posttraumatic stress disorder (PTSD) is the higher risk of this prolonged disorder in women. Their explanation reviewed within a psychobiological model of PTSD suggest that women's higher risk for this disorder may be due to the type of trauma they experience, their younger age at the time of trauma exposure, their stronger perceptions of threat and loss of control, higher levels of peritraumatic dissociation, insufficient social support resources and greater use of alcohol to manage trauma-related symptoms like intrusive memories and disassociation as well as gender-specific acute psychobiological reactions to trauma.

Complex post-traumatic symptomatic disease (CPTSD) consists of five different problem areas which are shown by research to be associated with early interpersonal trauma (Herman 1992a). These are alterations in the regulation of affective impulses, identity, insecure relationships, altered consciousness and somatization.

How can these disorders be best assessed, diagnosed and treated in children?

Haugaard (2004b) notes that children who are severely abused may be more likely than other children to persist in experiencing emotions through physical symptoms because of their history of the pairing of emotional trauma with physical trauma or pain. Common forms of somatization found in children are headaches, recurrent abdominal and limb pain. Furthermore, Diehl and Prout (2002) explain that a child who has been traumatized and sexually abused will especially have difficulty in attaining and maintaining an independent sense of self or self-efficacy. The fore-going suggests that psycho-therapists will need to assess symptoms carefully to arrive at accurate diagnoses of various disorders.

In assessment it is important to note that cultural factors are likely to play an integral role in the possible development of PTSD in maltreated and non-maltreated youth. Ferrari (2002) concludes that differences in parenting, for example disciplinary practices such as the use of physical punishment cannot be considered abusive or benign without a close up view of the entire family system. The child's resilience including the use of reasoning and nurturing behavior may serve to stave-off the possible harmful effects of physical punishment. Other researchers have examined maltreatment in poorer countries finding that poverty, stressful effects of migration, lack of information about child development, health care and disciplinary practices that are harmful to youths and other practices such as ritual and medical circumcision relate closely to trauma (Ramos and Boyle, 2000). How these factors specifically relate to PTSD development is yet unclear but some contemporary researchers have cited certain aspects of culture as having possible impact.

Laugharne, Lilee and Janca (2010) explain that recent research supports previous findings of high levels of comorbidity for PTSD and marked symptom overlap between this disorder, anxiety disorders and depressive disorders. They posit that accumulating evidence in regard to these issues should encourage clinicians to think of the potential relevance of trauma in the cause of anxiety disorders, other than PTSD and depressive disorders. These researchers believe that often a sub-syndromal partial PTSD is subsumed within another diagnosis. The relevance of this information points to the need for clinicians to take a detailed trauma history regarding re-experiencing, avoidance, numbing and hyperarousal symptoms during assessment.

Kaplow and Widom (2007) inform us that their findings from research conducted with adults who were abused between the ages of 0–11 years have important implications for assessment, prevention and intervention efforts targeting maltreated children. In their study they found it meaningful that the age of onset of maltreatment during childhood has a significant impact beyond adolescence into adulthood. They note that although previous studies have reported strong relationships between childhood maltreatment and psychopathology, the current study suggests differential effects of child maltreatment on the basis of the age of onset of the maltreatment. They believe that these findings could be used to develop more appropriate prevention strategies tailored to the age of onset of maltreatment. They agree that the preschool years appear to be a particularly sensitive developmental period with regard to the potential importance of maltreatment and subsequent effects namely adult anxiety, depression and anti-social personality disorder. Children identified as having experienced maltreatment during the preschool years might be prioritized over other groups for prevention efforts particularly in the case of limited resources. Interventions that focus on the acquisition of self-regulation skills or positive parent–child interactions may be particularly useful in this regard given the links between secure attachment relationships and self-regulation in the development of healthy psychological functioning.

McIntosh and Mata (2008) posit that the symptoms of PTSD differ substantially between children and adolescents and between children and adults. For example, children may engage in re-enactments of trauma which are more than likely to be articulated in play rather than through verbal communication. They believe that children are less likely to experience flashbacks than adults. These researchers state that psychosomatic complaints such as gastro-intestinal symptoms, headaches, sleep disturbance, concentration problems and anxiety are common complaints among children who have been traumatized and can be used in their assessment.

Briere and Lanktree (2008) state that a combination of a carefully selected psychological test battery along with other forms of information can help determine the extent of the adolescent's trauma-related symptomatology as well as any other psychological difficulties that may also be present. One such means of assessment is the children's PTSD inventory which is designed as a structured interview intended for assessment of post-traumatic stress disorder in children and adolescents between the ages of 6-18 years of age (Saigh, 2004). This author notes that one challenge is that this age range may contain a number of developmental stages with specific characteristics and complexities that may not be identical across the entire age-range.

With this brings the likelihood that scores might not meet empirical thresholds and could result in diagnoses for similar symptoms at different developmental stages.

A study by Lanktree, Gilbert, Briere, Taylor, Chen, Maida and Saltzman, (2008) reveal that the trauma symptom checklist for children (TSCC) and the trauma symptom checklist for young children (TSCYC) yielded a moderate correlation. At the same time, these different sources of information converged on most of the underlying symptoms assumed to exist or shared by both measures thus supporting each measure's discriminant validity. As a result of their study, these researchers suggest that when assessing trauma related symptomatology in children, both child and parent report measures should be used. Briere and Lanktree (2008) report on the UCLA PTSD Index for DSM-IV which is an updated version of what was formerly described as the Reaction Index which can be used for assessment of children; while the UPID is a 48-item interview that can be administered to children and adolescents aged 7-18 years. The UPID evaluates exposure to a variety of traumatic events and provides a PTSD diagnosis as well as containing additional items that assess associated features such as guilt, aggression and dissociation.

These various trauma-specific measures mentioned by Briere and Lanktree, (2008) are described here. It shows the trauma symptom checklist for children was normed on a population of over 3,000 across a range of socio-demographic strata. The 54-item TSCC evaluates post-traumatic symptomatology in children and adolescents ages 8-16 with minor normative adjustments for 17 year-olds including the effects of child abuse namely sexual, physical and psychological, neglect and other interpersonal violence, witnessing trauma, major accidents and disasters. The scale measures not only post-traumatic stress but also other symptom clusters found in some traumatized children. It has two validity scales and six clinical scales which are anxiety, depression, anger, post-traumatic stress and sexual concerns which contain two subscales namely distress and preoccupation and dissociation with two subscales: overt and fantasy. Briere and Lanktree explain that there is an alternate form; the TSCC-A which does not include any sexual items.

In a study by Feather and Ronan (2006) multiple abused children who were seen in a clinic in New Zealand were diagnosed with post-traumatic stress disorder (PTSD). Careful assessment was conducted by these authors to ascertain their levels of functioning prior to treatment. One instrument used in assessment was the anxiety disorders interview schedule for children (ADIS) by Silverman (1994). This structured clinical interview was administered to children with a parallel version for parents. This helped to increase rapport and enabled gathering of information on a child's historical and current functioning.

Another instrument used by these researchers is the state trait anxiety inventory for children (STAIC) by Speilberger (1973) which accurately measures trait and state anxiety in 9-12 year olds. Each scale has 20 items rated on a three-point Likert scale. The trait scale is treatment sensitive and can be used to measure the effectiveness of clinical procedures designed to reduce anxiety in children. Scores can range from 20-60 with higher scores indicating higher anxiety.

The third instrument used was the children's post-traumatic stress reaction index (CPTS-RI) by Fredrick, Pynoos and Nader (1992). This is a 20 item measure rated on a 5-point Likert scale (scored 0-4) that assesses the features and symptoms of PTSD in children. It is reported to be widely used in research and it can be administered in a self-report or interview format. Scores can range from 0-80, with a cut off of 12+ indicating a mild PTSD reaction; 25+ a moderate PTSD reaction and 40+ a severe PTSD reaction.

The fourth instrument used for assessment was the children's depression inventory (CDI) Kovas (1981). The CDI assesses affective, behavioral and cognitive signs of depression. It has 27 items with each item having three choices with scores from zero to two for children and adolescents aged 8-19 that measures the severity of depressive symptoms. Briere and Lanktree (2008) agree that standardized tests for specific symptoms or disorders include the child depression inventory CDI; and they name the suicidal ideation questionnaire SIQ, Reynolds 1988 and Tennessee self-concept Scale TSCS, Reid and Fitts 1994, as other useful measures.

The coping questionnaire (CQ)-C by Rendall, Chamsky, Kane Kortlander and Ronan (1992) measures the self-perceived coping ability of a child in specific anxiety-provoking situations, while the child behavior checklist/4-18 parent form (CBCL/4-18) Achenbach (1991a) measures parent/caregiver reports of child competencies. This latter instrument has two sections (a) social competencies and (b) problem behaviors. The final instrument used to assess children's problems and competencies in the realm of social/emotional functioning at school was the child behavior checklist–teacher's report form (TRF) Achenbach (1991b).

Goldfinch (2009) a proponent of family therapy, notes that it is best to work with the entire family to promote safety increasing an understanding and trust between members and will increase positive times/interaction together among family members. Other types of family therapy are dyadic therapy (DT) and parent-child interaction therapy (PCIT) which seeks to improve the parent-child relationship. In addition, this writer proposes that psycho-educational groups that teach positive discipline will help improve parenting skills. She posits that dialectical behavior therapy (DBT) and mindfulness can help parents take into consideration the way they respond to their children's actions. One behavior management strategy suggested by Goldfinch is by having children take a 'time out or take space.' She also suggests that building interpersonal skills and a sense of competence can be achieved through PALS by Wingecarribee Health Service (2003) or the use of circle time or fun friends by Barrett (2007).

Smith, Yule, Perrin, Tranah, Dalgleish and Clarke (2007) compared CBT to a waitlist control condition in 24 children and adolescents (8–18 years) exposed to single-event traumas. These traumas included motor vehicle accidents, assault or exposure to violence. The parents and youths were interviewed prior to their inclusion in the study. All youths met DSM-IV criteria for PTSD on the basis of the anxiety disorders interview schedule (child and parent versions) by Silverman and Albano, 1996. CBT was based on the cognitive model of Ehlers and Clark (2000) and adapted for youths although this was in some way similar to other CBT interventions (Smith et al., 2007). However, their use of CBT interventions emphasized more heavily than other interventions on the targeting of cognitive factors. These factors include disjointed and poorly elaborated trauma memories, misappraisals of trauma-related symptoms and dysfunctional coping strategies that are believed to maintain post traumatic stress (PTS) reactions. CBT in this study consisted of 10 weekly individual youth sessions and 10 individual parent sessions and joint parent-child sessions as needed. Results indicated significant improvements for CBT but not for the waitlist on all youth self-rating scales of PTSD on the children's attributions and perceptions scale [CAPS], Mannarino, Cohen, and Berman,1994; and children's revised impact of events scale, Perrin, Meiser-Stedman, & Smith, 2005, depression (i.e., depression self rating scale; Birleson, 1981) revised children's manifest anxiety scale RCMAS-2, Reynolds and Richmond 2008. Clinician-rated diagnostic status using the CAPS also improved significantly for the CBT group but not for the waitlist. Six-month follow-up data showed treatment gains for CBT were maintained on all measures.

By understanding the child's emotional experience and behavioral responses clinicians can devise effective treatment regimens which are relevant to the client's specific clinical presentation and needs. If assessment is repeated over time, it can highlight the need to change the treatment focus. For example, ongoing evaluation may suggest a shift in therapeutic focus when post-traumatic stress symptoms begin to respond to treatment but other symptoms continue.

The use of relative treatment protocols designed for infants, toddlers and young children specifically target the child care-giver dyad while protocols for complex trauma, particularly those for use with adolescents utilize a group therapy format to address skill development, affect regulation, interpersonal connection, competence and resiliency building (Cook, Spinazzola, Ford, Lanktree, Blaustein, Cloitre, DeRosa, Kagan, Liautaurd, Mallah, Olafson and Van der Kolk, 2005).

A randomized controlled trial trauma-focused group psychotherapy (TFGT) was compared with present-focused group psychotherapy (PFGF) and a waitlist condition for 166 survivors of childhood sexual abuse who were at risk for HIV infection (Walker, Reese, Hughes and Troskie, 2010). The clientele included persons who were at risk for HIV infection based on sexual revictimization, drug and alcohol use and risky sex as well as post-traumatic stress disorder (PTSD) symptoms. In this study, it was hypothesized that TFGP would be superior to the PFGP and waitlist conditions and that receiving both forms of treatment would be superior to no treatment (waitlist condition). Intention-to-treat analyses for HIV risk found all conditions reduced this risk of contracting HIV. Intention-to-treat analyses for PTSD symptoms found a reduction for all conditions but there was no advantage for using either TFGT in reducing PTSD symptoms. However, there was an effect for treatment compared with the waitlist condition. On secondary outcomes there was a greater reduction in anger for TFGT compared with PFGT when comparing treatment with the waitlist condition. This resulted in a greater reduction in hyper-arousal, re-experiencing, anger and impaired self-reference for the treatment condition. Adequate dose that is treatment analyses generally confirmed the intention-to-treat findings and additionally found that treatment led to reductions in depression, dissociation and sexual concerns.

Keeton and Ginsbury (2008) note there is an absence of data on the efficacy of combination therapy, that is psychosocial and medication for the treatment of anxiety disorders such as social phobia (SOP), generalized anxiety (GAD) and separation anxiety (SAD) in youths although clinicians often utilize this treatment approach. They cite Compton, Burns, Helen and Robertson, (2002) when stating that both cognitive behavioral therapy (CBT) and pharmacotherapy (PT) are efficacious interventions for over 50% of children and adolescents with social phobia (SOP), generalized anxiety (GAD) and separation anxiety (SAD).

They believe a substantial number of youths (20-45%) derive less than optimal gains from treatment. In their article, Keeton and Ginsbury (2008) discuss issues related to sequencing, combining and integrating cognitive behavioral and pharmacological interventions for anxiety disorders in children and adolescents. They provide an integrated treatment model to facilitate the delivery of a comprehensive treatment approach across care providers.

While comparing TF-CBT with school based group cognitive behavior treatment (TF-CBT), Silverman, Ortiz, Viswesvaran, Burns, Kolko, Putman and Amaya-Jackson, (2008) found that the former met the well established criteria for children and adolescents who have been exposed to traumatic events up to 1993–2007 while the latter met the criteria for probably efficacious treatment. All the other treatments were classified as either possibly efficacious or experimental. Whenever results of pre-tests and post-tests are used to compare the functioning of both children and adolescents before treatment and after, they show a positive impact of treatment on cognitive, emotional and behavioral functioning in subjects (Carew, 2007). In a study, Cohen and Mannarino (1996) compared CBT for sexually abused preschool children CBT-SAP; n ¼ 39 to nondirective supportive therapy NST; n ¼ 28 in 67 sexually abused children 2–7 years. CBT-SAP group continued to show maintenance in their reduction of inappropriate sexual behaviors using the child sexual behavior inventory (CSBI) with further statistically significant improvement found between the 6 and 12 month follow-ups. In addition, children in CBT-SAP continued to show maintenance in their reduction of inappropriate sexual behaviors using the CSBI, with further statistically significant improvements found between the 6 and 12 month follow-ups.

Pre to post-treatment comparisons showed statistically significant reductions for both child CBT and family CBT. These improvements were all maintained at 12 week follow-up with again no significant differences between child CBT and family CBT. TF-CBT was similar in content and duration to CBT-SAP used with preschool children by Cohen and Mannarino, (2004) with therapeutic strategies adapted for use with older children. TF-CBT showed significant improvements for PTSD at 12-month follow-up because children in TF-CBT continued to improve whereas those in non-directive supportive therapy (NST) did not.

In the treatment of the multiple abused children seen by Feather and Ronan (2006) mentioned earlier, they used a 65 page manual of TF-CBT program which comprised 16 structured sessions offered in four phases to children and their parent-caregivers. Phase one featured psychosocial strengthening and rapport building and orientation to therapy, the STAR plan and parent/caregiver's treatment. Phase two dealt with coping skills, while phase three dealt with trauma processing and phase four dealt with special issues and completion of therapy. The results showed that PTSD symptoms generally decreased and gains improved over 3, 6, and 12 months follow-ups.

Cohen and Mannarino (2008) report that the TF-CBT model used is a flexible, evidence-based treatment for traumatized children. It has been tested in several completed and ongoing studies for children and adolescents aged 3–17 years old who have experienced sexual abuse, traumatic grief, domestic violence, terrorism, disasters and multiple traumatic events. It is currently being adapted and tested for use internationally. A study by Silverman, et al. (2008) noted that the results of an analysis of children and adolescents exposed to trauma met the diagnosis for PTSD. They also found that only TF-CBT met the criteria of well-established treatment for these two age groups.

The TF-CBT approach evaluated in a study conducted by Cohen, Berliner, Mannarino and Steer (2004) found this treatment to be more effective in treating PTSD and to be superior to child centered therapy (CCT) in reducing abuse-related attributions and shame. They also found it to be effective in reducing parallel depression and parental distress regarding their children's sexual abuse and served to enhance parental support of the child and other positive parenting practices. This study is believed to further support the use of TF-CBT in treating multiply traumatized sexually abused children.

Child-based treatments of PTSD using CBT include psycho-education, imaginal exposure, in-vivo exposure, coping skills, relaxation training, behavior rehearsal, cognitive therapy, assertiveness training, graded exposure and relapse prevention. Family-based treatments additionally include parent training in behavior management and communication skills. Treatments are equally effective and better than control especially with respect to fear, anxiety and global functioning. Dalgleish, Meiser-Stedman and Smith (2005) and Stirling and Amaya-Jackson (2008) also found that a cognitive-behavioral approach to be effective for children and youths with PTSD who had been assaulted or abused. This approach includes education about child abuse and common childhood reactions, safety skills, stress management techniques, emotion regulation, creating a coherent narrative of the event and facilitating appropriate emotional and cognitive processing. These researchers recommend the inclusion of dyadic and co-joint parent work and continuing therapy with children especially younger preverbal ones. Avinger and Jones (2007) and Cohen and Mannarino (2004) note that trauma focused CBT is useful in addressing symptoms of PTSD in youths while other youth groups treated with psychodrama show significant decreases in depression and increases in self-esteem. Avinger and Jones (2007) state that girls who have been victims of child sexual abuse (CSA) and engaged in Humanistic/Rogerian group treatment experienced alleviation of self-reported anxiety.

Jaycox, Langley, Stein, Wong, Sharma, Scott and Schonlau (2009) evaluated 'support for students exposed to trauma' (SSET) adapted from the cognitive behavior intervention for trauma in Schools (CBITS) program. Results of this pilot study demonstrated that the program can be implemented successfully by teachers and counselors with good results among students and parents. The results showed small reductions of trauma in students in this program, indicating promise that warrants a full evaluation of effectiveness. Jaycox, et al. (2010) provide details about treatments given to children who were assessed and found to be traumatized. One is cognitive-behavioral intervention for trauma in schools CBITS which uses a 10-group session and between 1–3 individual session(s) intervention. This program which is designed specifically for use in schools has been successful with children of many different cultural groups and those who have suffered multiple forms of trauma. However, there are also significant differences between these two models, TF-CBT are provided in conjoint sessions (with parent and child) whereas CBITS is provided in a group format for children only.

Lieberman, Van-Horn and Ippen (2005) compared child-parent psychotherapy (CPP) and case management in 65 young children (3–5 years) who had witnessed or overheard marital violence. CPP applied clinical strategies and clinical illustrations to address the following domains of functioning: play, sensorimotor disorganization and disruption of biological rhythms, fearfulness, recklessness, self endangering and accident prone behavior, aggression, punitive and critical parenting as well as the relationship with the perpetrator of the violence and or absent father. Case management involved monthly telephone contact with the mothers as well as providing information about local mental health clinics including referrals. Pre to post-treatment comparisons revealed statistically significant improvements for cerebral perfusion pressure, but not on case management using the CBCL-Total subscale and when the post-traumatic stress symptom scale for children (PTSS) was utilized as a semi-structured interview. Therefore, CBCL may be best used as a screening rather than diagnostic tool (Hulette, 2008).

Integrative family therapy (IFT) includes sessions with the child or children who are traumatized focusing on identifying the reasons why they are hesitant to be open with caregivers and by helping them to articulate this hesitation (Sheinberg and True, 2008). This involves the recursive process of going from a family session and returning to individual sessions to increase relational information and opportunities for therapeutic intervention. These researchers report that minority representation is relatively higher in this area than in many other areas of child and adolescent treatment research. However, lacking in these studies are detailed explanations as to how they adapted or modified their treatment programs to ensure the treatment was sensitively attuned to the cultural context of the minority group making it more attractive than the non-culturally attuned treatments. As previously noted, the inclusion of heterogeneous ethnic samples in treatments significantly decreased the effects. Overall this type of work is critical in providing answers as to why treatments work and for whom. Such work would lead to improved transportability of evidence-based treatments because knowledge progresses about what is most responsible for change. Hence, treatments can be tailored to meet the needs of specific groups attending mental health clinics. For example a topic worthy of further examination is the role of parental involvement in treatment in relation to child improvement.

Another treatment model reported to be effective or evidence based is filial therapy. In this form of therapy parents are taught play therapy skills enabling them to assist their children in dealing with emotional and behavioral problems in the context of parental empathy and validation (Topham, Wampler, Titus and Rolling, 2011). These writers report that filial therapy is offered in several different formats including the original group format developed by the Guerneys, 1964. This is a short-term group format adapted by Garry Landreth and Sue Bratton, 2006 and referred to as child parent relationship therapy (CPRT), and an individual family therapy model adapted by Rise and VanFleet, Sywulak and Sniscak, 1994.

Treatments promising effective results have been found for maltreated youths with symptoms of PTSD. In particular eye movement desensitization and reprocessing (EMDR) originally designed for adults with PTSD is considered as one such treatment even though early work indicate it's utility for maltreated children with PTSD. Ahmad, Larsson and Sundelin-Wahlsten (2007) report that eight sessions of EDMR for children with PTSD, many of whom had experienced maltreatment produced markedly less PTSD symptoms than controls for re-experiencing symptoms and avoidance. This data supports other preliminary work using EMDR for adolescents with PTSD as possibly effective (Silverman et al., 2008). Tufnell (2005) adds that EMDR can be adapted for use as part of a multimodal treatment package for PTSD for both pre-adolescents and adolescents.

Other treatments have been introduced for youths with PTSD who have been maltreated. For example residential trauma-focused treatment (RT-FT) consists of a short-term approach focusing on safety, affect modulation, anxiety management, problem solving and empathy, addressing personal loss and pro-social interpersonal relationships. A trauma recovery treatment model is used to teach youths effective adaptation and coping skills to replace non-adaptive cognitive and social behavioral strategies. A key goal is to help youths move from victimization to self-efficacy and reduce their trauma-related symptoms (Rivard, Bloom, McCorkle and Abramovitz, 2005). Egeland (2009) calls for extension of these and other related cognitive-behavioral strategies to home and community based treatments for maltreated youths with trauma symptoms. Lawson (2009) notes that although the specifics of treatment effectiveness have yet to be sorted out research does indicate that any mode of established treatment is superior to no treatment for maltreated children. CBT and family/parent models have been shown to be the most effective types of treatment when a number of studies are done. He explains that counselors must consider the severity and frequency of the trauma, age of the victim, parent/family support and dosage of treatment in implementing appropriate therapy for each case.

 Caffo and Belaise (2007) agree with Margolin and Vickerman (2007) that a significant proportion of trauma occurs in children which incur severe psychological distress after traumatic events that interfere with their social and family relationships. These foremost psychiatric problems following traumatic experiences include delayed development, learning disorders, post-traumatic stress disorder, anxiety, mood disorders, sleep disorders, conduct disorder and attention deficit disorders. Copeland, Keeper, Angold and Costello (2007) add that higher levels of traumatic exposure were related to higher levels of most psychopathologies including anxiety disorders. One example of this is experiencing the unexpected death of a peer which is a traumatic event that has been related to symptoms of PTSD, intrusive thoughts, persistent anger, depression, anxiety disorders and emotional suppression and other impairments. Kearney, et al. (2009) explain that depression is a primary gateway for precursor symptoms that leads to PTSD in maltreated youths. Others have found that maltreated children with PTSD and depression report greater levels of intrusive PTSD related symptoms than those with PTSD only. These might include re-living, flashbacks, re-enactment, amnesia and sleep problems.

Childhood traumatic grief (CTG) refers to a condition in which a child or adolescent has lost a loved one through circumstances that are said to be objectively or subjectively traumatic and in which trauma symptoms interfere with the normal grieving process (Cohen and Mannarino, 2004). These researchers believe that it is not normative for children to experience persistent trauma symptoms as part of the grief process even if the loss occurs in the context of trauma. Other studies on grief associated with trauma have reported similarities between adult and adolescent grief.

After examining data on child and parent report of acute stress disorder (ASD) or PTSD, Meiser-Stedman, Smith, Gluckman and Yule (2007) conclude that children were significantly more likely to meet criteria for ASD and PTSD symptom clusters based on their own report than on their parent's report. Based on this, these authors believe that if parents or caregivers are able to recognize post-traumatic stress in their children's parents or caregivers this may be the appropriate point of assessment in the aftermath of trauma.

O'Donnell, Joshi and Lewin (2007) refer readers to a number of fact-sheets on-line at www.dcchildrens.com/ichoc. These can guide parents, teachers and even clinicians in providing psychosocial support for children who have been exposed to traumatic stressful events such as wars, shootings, earthquakes and storms. This source suggests that expressive therapies such as play, art and music could be used for children. They also give details on other ways adults can be present with children to allay ASD and PTSD.

McIntosh and Mata (2008) agree with the fore-going discussion. They state that a literature review suggesting developmentally sensitive assessment of symptoms after trauma may be more valid than the Diagnostic and Statistical Manual of Mental Disorders, 4th. ed. DSM 1V criteria because symptoms of PTSD differ substantially between children and adults. These researchers suggest that many children are under-diagnosed due to the utilization of current DSM-IV criteria. Dalgleish, Meiser-Stedman, Kassam-Adams, Ehlers, Winston, Smith, Bryant, Mayou and Yule (2008) say that whether or not children exhibit symptoms of PTSD, they have developed in the context of ongoing danger, maltreatment and inadequate care-giving systems which are ill-served by the current diagnostic system as it frequently leads to no diagnosis, multiple unrelated diagnoses, an emphasis on behavioral control without recognition of interpersonal trauma and lack of safety in the etiology of symptoms and a lack of attention to ameliorating the developmental disruptions that underlie the symptoms.

Dalgleish et al. proposed a diagnostic criterion based on a brief review of published and unpublished data rationale and assessment of the reliability and validity data as well as the justification for meeting the criteria for creating a new diagnosis in the DSM V which was actually released in May 2013. Prior to this happening Vander Kolk, et al. (2009) wrote about the goal of the National Child Traumatic Stress Network to introduce the diagnosis of developmental trauma disorder which intended to capture the reality of the clinical presentations of children and adolescents exposed to chronic interpersonal trauma. This would serve to guide clinicians in developing effective interventions and for researchers to study the neurobiology and transmission of chronic interpersonal violence. This diagnosis will serve to replace the diagnosis of PTSD for some youths which does not adequately capture the symptoms of children who are victims of interpersonal violence in the context of inadequate care-giving systems.

Bendall, Jackson, Hulbert and McGory (2008) in a review of the literature show the importance of paying attention to the methodology of studies of child trauma and psychosis. They highlight the need for appropriate control groups to be used in experiments for establishing meaningful associations between child trauma and psychosis. They also note there are problems associated with lack of large-scale prospective studies which would provide the most robust results. Innovative methodologies may be able to investigate the relationship in different ways such as empirically testing theorized relationships between child trauma and psychosis. For example in one study of a group with schizophrenia, diurnal cortisol secretion was found to be different than those with a history of child trauma compared with those without, supporting the theory that child trauma is associated with schizophrenia through hypothalamic-pituitary-adrenal axis dysregulation. They note there is the possibility that child trauma is associated with an atypical form of psychosis characterized by hallucinations and delusions. These researchers suggest though that psychosis diagnosis and symptomatology should be investigated more thoroughly.

In a study by Mathews, Nirmaljct and Stein (2008) they concluded that obsessive compulsive disorder could be linked with childhood trauma. However, these researchers believe that the relationship between childhood trauma and obsessive-compulsive symptoms has not been well studied. In their most recent study it examines the relationship between childhood trauma, personality facets and obsessive-compulsive symptoms in 938 college students using the Childhood Trauma Questionnaire, the Leyton Obsessional Inventory and the NEO Personality Inventory Revised. Between 13% and 30% of the subjects met the criteria for childhood trauma with emotional neglect being the most commonly reported experience. They found there was a small but significant association between obsessive-compulsive symptoms and childhood trauma in particular emotional abuse and physical neglect, all of which were accounted for by co-occurring anxiety symptoms. An independent association was also seen between emotional abuse, physical abuse and high levels of obsessive compulsive symptoms which remained significant in the context of co-occurring anxiety symptoms. These researchers found a similar association between obsessive-compulsive symptoms and conscientiousness and between emotional neglect and sexual abuse and conscientiousness, suggesting that an indirect role for childhood trauma in the development of obsessive compulsive symptoms may also exist.

Dalgleish, Meiser-Stedman and Smith (2005) welcome the inclusion of a cognitive component in behavioral therapy which has been successful in several treatment outcome studies for maltreated youths and/or youths with PTSD. Primary treatment goals using CBT are to help children overcome intense shame, guilt and anxiety regarding abusive experiences. Cohen, et al. (2004) explains that trauma focused cognitive behavioral therapy is a treatment that partially focuses on recognizing relationships between thoughts, behaviors, emotions and cognitive processing of abuse experiences and developing trauma narratives and coping skills.

In assessing trauma in children, experimental paradigms have shown individuals with PTSD are faster to respond to threat meanings of homographs, which are words with two meanings more than traumatized individuals without PTSD (Amir, Coles and Foa, 2002). Huppert, Foa, McNally and Cahill (2011) explain the misinterpretation of positive stimuli could be important to the development and maintenance of PTSD reflecting a negative interpretation bias.

Primary interventions in this regard and for PTSD in particular include debriefing as well as cognitive behavioral, art, play, psychodynamic and pharmacological therapies. Bratton, Ray, Rhine and Jones (2005) assert play therapy is a developmentally responsive intervention widely used by child therapists but often criticized for lacking an adequate research base to support its growing practice. A meta-analysis of 93 controlled outcome studies published between 1953 and 2000 was conducted to assess the overall efficacy of play therapy and to determine factors that might impact its effectiveness. The overall treatment effect for play therapy interventions was 0.80 standard deviations. Further analysis revealed that effects were more positive for humanistic than for non-humanistic treatments and using parents in play therapy produced the largest effects. Play therapy appeared equally effective across age, gender and presenting issue.

Parents and youths in maltreatment cases often differ with respect to information provided, which may reflect self-interest or legal ramifications. Such ramifications can also influence consent to assessment and treatment (Carter-Visscher, Naugle, Bell and Suvak, 2007). These researchers report maltreated youths may be less likely to speak to an assessor about their trauma in the presence of a parent. Eye movement desensitization and reprocessing (EMDR) was originally designed for adults with PTSD though some early work indicates its utility for maltreated children with PTSD. This data support other preliminary work regarding EMDR for adolescents with PTSD and the treatment has been described as possibly efficacious (Silverman et al., 2008).

Kearney, et al. (2008) relate that specific youth based techniques include structured play, expressing maltreatment-related feelings of fear, anxiety management and changing erroneous beliefs of self-blame and negative attributions about others, teaching maltreatment prevention skills and reducing isolation and stigma associated with maltreatment, as in group therapy. An emphasis on parents includes reducing psychopathological symptoms such as depression as well as dysfunctional parenting practices. Family-based approaches to access community resources, increase cohesion and reduces conflict and associated child behavior problems are commonly employed as well. Broader peer counseling and community programs have also been advocated especially for cases involving domestic violence.

Koverola, Murtaugh, Connors, Reeves and Papas (2007) and Markese (2007) explain speed of recovery is often dictated by degree of child resilience, parental support and responsiveness, maternal distress, family help-seeking, family cohesion and age appropriate therapeutic interventions. Ross and O'Carrol (2004) conclude that contrary to concerns expressed by clinicians, sexually abused children and their non-abusing care-givers can significantly benefit from cognitive behavioral interventions which use reliving and confrontation of the abusive experience.

The neurobiology of PTSD has provided us with growing evidence of the negative impact traumatic life events have on children's brain development and functioning and has suggested intriguing therapeutic possibilities for traumatized children. These researchers suggest that more research is needed to test these potential treatments particularly pharmacologic therapies when administered both alone and in combination for children with a variety of trauma-related symptoms. They further recommend more effort be placed on training practitioners in those interventions that already have evidence of effectiveness. Additionally, several changes in policy and funding are needed in order to optimize treatment for traumatized children.

In keeping with this view several researchers have begun to develop a comprehensive framework for treatment based on cognitive-behavioral principles. These treatments largely focus on altering the learning experiences that lead from stressor to PTSD symptoms, reducing anxiety so a youth can adequately process strong negative emotions and trauma-related thoughts enhancing self-regulation and positive affect. It is useful working with a non-offending parent to boost support and decrease distress while improving positive parenting practices, especially those related to discipline. Those treatments use a group therapy format to address skill development, affect regulation, interpersonal connection and resiliency training when working with adolescents (Cohen, Mannarino, Murray, Ingelman, 2006; Cook et al., 2005, Ross and O'Carroll, 2004).

A popular model of treatment for maltreated youths with PTSD is trauma-focused cognitive behavioral therapy (TF-CBT) that focuses poignantly on education regarding child maltreatment especially sexual abuse, using coping skills training, gradual exposure and parent-based techniques. This information is based on the work of Cohen, Deblinger, Mannarino and Steer (2004) and Heflin and Deblinger (2006). A general goal of this treatment is to help the non-offending parent act as a future therapeutic agent for the youth and ease symptoms of depression, PTSD and affect dysregulation.

These researchers describe this approach as including 12–20 sessions during which a youth is initially provided education about what abuse is and why it occurs, who is responsible for the abuse, frequency of abuse, what types of youths are abused, how youth feel when abused and why youths often find it difficult to tell others of abuse. Apart from education, this process allows a child to have initial general discussions about maltreatment experiences and PTSD symptoms. Inaccurate and particularly distressful perceptions about these experiences and symptoms can be addressed at this point and later during journaling. Coping skills training focuses on linking thoughts, emotions and behaviors for a child to illustrate their inter-relational effects. In addition, cognitive therapy is designed for maltreatment and non-maltreatment situations to identify thoughts that underlie strong emotions such as guilt and evaluate the utility and accuracy of thoughts in these scenarios to generate more adaptive and realistic thoughts.

Journaling key thoughts and emotions and role playing to develop skills for appropriate emotional expression are important aspects of coping skills training. Exposure-based practices involve hierarchies of stimuli related to intense anxiety surrounding a set of maltreatment experiences. Examples of hierarchy items include discussions of maltreatment in general, one's relationship with family members including an offender, less stressful maltreatment experiences and specific and detailed descriptions of the most serious offenses. Youths are encouraged to refrain from distraction and engage in emotional expression and cognitive coping skills during the exposure process. The use of written work in the form of diaries, journals, books, letters and essays is encouraged as well. Parent-based practices involve many of these same techniques for the non-offending parent who must provide support for a maltreated youth. A particular focus may be placed on depression and unrealistic expectations regarding one's interpersonal and familial relationships.

Parenting skills are emphasized to focus on appropriate disciplinary strategies, conflict resolution, handling strong adolescent emotions such as anger and providing education about dating, sexuality and body safety to one's children. It is believed that didactic discussions with a youth and parent regarding potentially dangerous situations in the future and what to do if re-victimization occurs are also helpful. Further descriptions can be found in Cohen and Mannarino's work published in 2008.

Hirai and Clum (2005) compared the efficacy of an 8-week internet-based self-help CBT program when applied to participants with subclinical symptomatology induced by a traumatic encounter and when assigned to a wait-list condition. The intervention comprised of CBT modules including: psycho-educational information, relaxation, cognitive restructuring and exposure, all delivered on the internet without face-to-face contact with the therapist. Results have proven that compared to the waitlist condition, participants receiving this intervention manifested significant decreases in avoidance behavior, frequency of intrusive thoughts, levels of anxiety and depressive symptoms. At the same time data revealed that these participants more frequently used adaptive coping skills than the participants in the waitlist condition.

Gewirtz, et al. (2008) state that the twin goals of parenting-based intervention following mass trauma would be to support parents in providing a social environment with structure, security and emotional warmth that addresses the traumatic event. In view of this goal, these researchers recommend the use of Patterson's time effective positive parenting practices promoting healthy child development, skill encouragement, limit setting, monitoring, interpersonal problem solving and positive involvement. These five core parenting skills are known as the parent management training Oregon-model (PMTO) for families with a high risk for varying levels of externalizing behaviors, including teenagers living in high crime neighborhoods and court adjudicated youngsters who are placed outside of their home receiving treatment.

Classen, Cavanaugh, Kaupp, Aggarwal, Palesh, Koopman, Kraemer and Spiegel (2011) report on a randomized controlled trial which compared trauma-focused group psychotherapy (TFGT) with present focused group psychotherapy (PFGT) and a waitlist condition for 166 survivors of childhood sexual abuse who were at risk for HIV infection. These persons included persons at risk for HIV infection based on sexual revictimization, drug and alcohol use and risky sex and post-traumatic stress disorder (PTSD) symptoms. When an intention-to-treat analyses for HIV risk was done it was found that all conditions reduced risk for other factors but there was no effect for HIV risk. However, intention-to-treat analyses for PTSD symptoms found a reduction for all conditions. The findings revealed there was no advantage for either TFGT or PFGT in reducing PTSD symptoms. On secondary outcomes, there was a greater reduction in anger for TFGT compared with PFGT and when treatment was compared with the waitlist condition. There was a greater reduction in hyper-arousal, re-experiencing, anger and impaired self-reference for those who were treated with either TFGT or PFGT. When an adequate dose analyses was done it generally confirmed the intention-to-treat findings and additionally found that treatment led to reductions in depression, dissociation and sexual concerns.

These authors relate that TF-CBT is a 12-session individual or conjoint intervention that includes child and parent and typically is delivered in clinics. TF-CBT has demonstrated effectiveness in improving PTSD and other symptoms in children experiencing sexual abuse, multiple trauma and disaster in multiple randomized trials. TF-CBT includes cognitive-behavioral skills, psycho-education, relaxation skills, affective modulation skills, cognitive coping skills, trauma narrative, in vivo mastery of trauma reminders and enhancing safety. TF-CBT is described as a hybrid treatment model integrating cognitive, behavioral, interpersonal and family therapy principles with trauma sensitive interventions for traumatized children and parents (Cohen, et al. 2006).

Child–parent psychotherapy is used to address sensorimotor disorganization and disruption of parenting, biological rhythms, fearfulness, recklessness, self-endangering and accident prone behavior, aggression, punitive and critical parenting as well as the relationship with the perpetuator (Lieberman, Van-Horn and Ippin, 2005). The treatment manual includes clinical strategies and clinical illustrations to address the following domains of functioning: play, sensorimotor disorganization, disruption of biological rhythms, fearfulness, recklessness, self-endangering, accident-prone behavior, aggression, punitive critical parenting and the relationship with the perpetrator of the violence and/or absent father.

Treatment research about interventions to reduce harm from trauma in youth has flourished in recent years. Primary interventions in this regard and for PTSD in particular include debriefing as well as cognitive-behavioral, art, play, psychodynamic and pharmacological therapies. More specific approaches include psycho-education, hypnotherapy, grief work, affect regulation, interpersonal skills development, narrative storytelling, coping skills and stress inoculation training, school consultation and exposure-based practices either individually or in group format. To date cognitive-behavioral approaches demonstrate the best efficacy especially for trauma related symptoms associated with anxiety and mood disorders. Wethington, Hahn, Fugua-

Whitely, Sipe, Crosby, Johnson, Liberman, Moscicki, Price, Tuma, Farris, Katra and Chattopadhyay (2008) believe when treatment is provided it could be improved on by adding a greater emphasis on the use of training and the use of evidence-based practices such as CBT.

Safety issues such as ongoing maltreatment or proximity to an abuser must be resolved immediately as well. Smith, Yule, Perrin, Tranah, Dalgleish and Clarke (2007) report at present there is general consensus among trauma experts that CBT in the form of prolonged therapeutic exposure and cognitive restructuring is the first-line treatment for PTSD in children and adolescents. At the same time Stein, Ipser, and McAnda (2009) report pharmacotherapy is not recommended for very young children. They do note that several clinical guidelines recommend that some SSRIs namely fluoxetine, paroxetine, sertraline and venlafaxine XR are appropriate first-line treatment approaches to PTSD for older children.

Crawford-Brown (1999) reports that some children in Jamaica who have been abused have been diagnosed with conduct disorder then subsequently placed in public institutions that care for them. She notes that previous studies showed that the interactional effects of the absence of fathers or low contact with them, absence of mother and the overall presence of negative parental role-models as contributory factors to conduct disorder in children.

Efforts to prevent violence among youths in Jamaica are reported in a documentation of interpersonal violence prevention programs for children published by the Caribbean Child Development Centre at the University of the West Indies, Mona (2005). The reports show there were 37 youth programs using preventive approaches dealing with the risk factors of different types of violence operating throughout the island targeting youths between the ages of 13-18 years. Crawford-Brown (1999) noted the need for a comprehensive re-tooling of staff training as well as a comprehensive treatment program to meet the special needs of children in institutions.

Writing about the paucity of mental health personnel who treat children exclusively in Jamaica, Shetty a child psychiatrist based at the Kingston Health Department told a reporter during an interview published in the Sunday Gleaner of May 29, 2011 that more than 90% of children with mental health issues are undiagnosed and untreated. He said, out of 100,000 children in need of help only 6,000 are seen annually. Shetty also bemoans that only 10 persons are employed by the Ministry of Health specializing exclusively in children's mental health issues and these employees are shared among the 20 child guidance clinics island wide.

How can these disorders be best assessed, diagnosed and treated in adolescents?

Some instruments are available to assess additional issues related to PTSD in adolescents. Due to the often elusive nature of dissociation a structured interview is often useful. Four are currently available:

The Structured Clinical Interview for DSM–IV Dissociation Disorders SCID-D by Steinberg 1994, which is the only interview with psychometric properties.

The Office Mental Status Examination for Complex Chronic Dissociative Symptoms.

Multiple Personality Disorder by Loewenstein 1991.

The Dissociative Disorders Interview Schedule DDIS by Ross, et al. 1989.

Results of these assessment instruments and interviews can guide the treatment process. Based on the information published by The United States Department of Veterans Affairs at gov/professional/pages/assess, the UCLA Index for DSM-1V (UPID) trauma symptom review for adolescents (TSRA) is a revision of the child PTSD reaction index CPTS-RI. Based on the information provided, these instruments are available for the assessment of all adolescents aged 12–21.

The trauma symptom inventory taps the overall level of post-traumatic symptomatology experienced by adolescents ages 18 to 21. It has three validity scales and 10 clinical scales; anxious arousal, depression, anger/irritability, intrusive experiences, defensive, avoidance, dissociation, sexual concerns, dysfunctional sexual behavior, impaired self-reference and tension reduction behavior.

Another instrument used in assessment is the detailed assessment of post-traumatic stress (DAPS) which is appropriate for use with adolescents 18 years of age and older. The DAPS has two validity scales and 10 scales that evaluate lifetime exposure to traumatic events: immediate, cognitive, emotional and dissociative responses to a specified traumatic event, the subsequent symptoms and diagnoses of PTSD and acute stress disorder (ASD) as well as three associated features of post-traumatic stress: trauma-specific dissociation, suicidality and substance abuse. The inventory of altered self-capacities (IASC) is a standardized test of difficulties in the areas of relatedness, identity and affect regulation. The scales are interpersonal conflicts, idealization, disillusionment, abandonment concerns, identity, impairment, susceptibility to influence, affect dysregulation and tension reduction activities.

As such it is especially relevant to the concerns and presentations of older adolescents between the ages of 18 to 21 with more complex post-traumatic outcomes. The trauma symptom review for adolescents (TSRA) was developed specifically to tap the major issues of traumatized adolescents aged 12 to 21. It has scales measuring among other constructs: trauma exposure, post-traumatic stress, attachment issues, dissociation, sexual issues, social isolation, tension-reduction, acting-out behaviors and vulnerability to revictimization. These authors note this instrument is currently undergoing standardization trials.

The two most useful instruments in the identification of CPTSD are the structured interview for disorders of extreme stress (SIDES) developed for the DSM–IV field trial and the trauma symptom inventory (TSI) developed to assess trauma symptoms (Pelcovitz, Van der Kolk, Roth, Mandel, Kaplan and Resick 1997) . They report that SIDES can be a useful tool for the investigation of alterations in response to extreme stress not currently captured by the PTSD diagnosis. It is also helpful in eliciting information regarding the effects of trauma and is particularly valuable in identifying areas of psychological impairment which is essential for effective treatment planning.

Briere and Lanktree (2008) provide a list of assessment measures used to assess trauma in adolescents. One of these is the integrated treatment for complex trauma (ITCT) which allows the clinician to assess various difficulties in a relatively structured way and is customizable to the specific clinical presentation and needs of the individual adolescent client. When engaging in ITCT assessment it typically includes information from a number of sources including the adolescent self-report, care-taker reports of his or her functioning, collateral reports from caregivers, teachers and other providers as well as psychological testing. The focus of assessment is the adolescent trauma exposure history and current psychological functioning or problems.

A standardized trauma-specific self-report measure for children and adolescents can be divided into those for youth ages 12–17, i.e. the trauma symptom checklist for children TSCC which can be divided in two groups ages 8-16 with normative adjustments for 17 year olds (Briere, 1996). Larkin and Read (2008) explain that whatever etiological model one adopts a large number of youths experience excessive traumatic experiences including physical, sexual and emotional abuse. These are precursors to adult psychosis, including schizophrenia, depression, anxiety disorders, substance abuse, eating disorders, post-traumatic stress disorder (PTSD), sexual dysfunction, personality disorders and suicidality. Based on these outcomes, they recommend that clinicians routinely inquire about trauma and abuse when they help people experiencing schizophrenia and other psychotic or unusual distressing situations. They believe it is essential to routinely assess for childhood and subsequent trauma when assisting people who report experiencing psychotic or psychotic-like phenomena. The growing theoretical understanding of the biological and psychosocial paths which may lead from trauma to psychosis can lead to an integrative approach to assessment, conceptualization and treatment which values psychological, social and biological interventions.

Research about interventions to reduce harm from trauma in youths has flourished in recent years. In view of this Solomon and Johnson (2002) reiterate the necessity of selecting the theoretical frameworks addressing the vast and varied needs of trauma survivors which is vital to a positive therapeutic experience. In view of this, these researchers acknowledge that cognitive-behavioral insight oriented approaches are emphasized as they are the most developed and researched approaches for the treatment of PTSD.

Courtis (2008) differentiates between individuals exposed to trauma over an expanse of time and developmental periods who suffer from a variety of psychological problems not included in the diagnosis of PTSD. These include depression, anxiety, self-hatred, dissociation, substance abuse, self-destructive and risk-taking behaviors, revictimization, problems with interpersonal and intimate relationships including parenting, medical, somatic concerns and despair. Moreover, these problems are categorized as comorbid conditions rather than being recognized as essential elements of complicated post-traumatic adaptations.

Furthermore, Courtis (2004) notes clinicians are discovering these complex conditions are extremely difficult to treat depending on the age and stage at which the trauma occurred, the relationship to the perpetrator of the trauma, the complexity of the trauma itself and the victim's role if any, the duration and objective seriousness of the trauma and the support received at the time and later on. Due to these differentiations, researchers involved in this work proposed an alternative conceptualization, Complex PTSD (CPTSD) for disorders of extreme stress not otherwise specified DESNOS (Pelcovitz, et al. 1997). According to Cook, et al. (2005) the primary self-endangering behavior seen in adolescents suffering from complex trauma exposure include suicidal, intentional but non-suicidal self-injury, major substance abuse, eating disorders, dysfunctional sexual behavior, excessive risk-taking and involvement in physical altercations. So the history of the individual should be considered when assessment of trauma is being done.

Meiser-Stedman, Smith, Bryant, Salmon, Yule, Dalgeish and Nixon (2009) explain there is a need to conduct research on empirically validated means of assessing trauma-exposed children and adolescents for the occurrence of PTSD. A measure of negative trauma-related cognitions for use with children and adolescents, the child post-traumatic cognitions inventory (CPTCI) is suggested as one instrument to fill the gap. The measure was devised as an age-appropriate version of the adult post-traumatic cognitions inventory (Meiser-Stedman et al., 2009). The CPTCI was developed by Foa, Ehlers, Clark, Tolin and Orsillo 1999 and validated within a large (n-570) sample comprising community and trauma-exposed samples of children and adolescents aged 6–18 years.

The principal components analysis suggested a two-component structure. These components were labeled 'permanent and disturbing change' and 'fragile person in a scary world.' Each was found to possess good internal consistency, test-retest reliability, convergent validity and discriminative validity. The reliability and validity of these sub-scales were present regardless of whether the measure was completed in the acute phase or several months after a trauma. Scores on these sub-scales did not vary with age.

It was then concluded that the CPTCI is a reliable and valid measure that is not specific to the type of trauma exposure and shows considerable promise as a research and clinical tool. The structure of this measure suggests appraisals concerning the more abstract consequences of a trauma as well as physical threat and vulnerability which are pertinent factors in trauma-exposed children and adolescents. In view of this Dalgleish, et al. (2008) proposed the introduction of the diagnosis of developmental trauma disorder in the DSM V, which is aimed at capturing the reality of the clinical presentations of children and adolescents exposed to chronic interpersonal trauma thereby guiding clinicians to develop and utilize effective interventions. The aim of introducing this system is to assist researchers in studying the neurobiology and transmission of chronic interpersonal violence.

Adaptations in methods and measures of assessment and interpretations may be necessary for multicultural groups within a country (Nader, 2007). A few individuals have developed assessment measures for some groups so testing can become routine in these populations. One such instance is an assessment instrument done by Edwards (2005) for Jamaican adolescents who have been maltreated. His doctoral thesis contains details of an instrument named the adolescent maladaptive scale (AMS) which can be used for screening of mild and severe behavioral problems and for diagnosing conduct disorder in the Jamaican context. He says this instrument is currently used by the Jamaican Ministry of Education in the assessment of adolescents aged 12–17 years to determine the levels of behavioral disorders and to place them in treatment programs.

Johnson and Coley (2008) suggest psychological assessments are routinely conducted in the Caribbean and especially in Jamaica at this time. These include intellectual, personality, behavioral and neuropsychological assessments. These authors note that despite the limited research that exists on the validity of psychological tests used in the Caribbean, the results have been promising and have some degree of cross-cultural applicability.

Regarding the need for treatment of adolescents with PTSD, Ahrens and Rexford (2002) compared cognitive processing therapy (CPT) to a waitlist condition of a sample of incarcerated male adolescents 15–18 years with PTSD. CPT involved eight one-hour sessions including psycho-education about PTSD by having the adolescents provide taped or written narratives of their thoughts and feelings at the time of the traumatic event and teaching them cognitive strategies. Results indicated that CPT showed statistically significant greater improvement than the waitlist condition on all three outcome measures based on the Beck Depression Inventory; Beck, Ward, Mendelson, Mock, and Erbaugh, 1961; Impact of Events Scale; Horowitz, Wilner and Alvarez, 1979 and PTSD symptom scale-self report; Foa, Riggs, Dancu, and Rothbaum, 1993, with no improvement for the waitlist.

In a study done by Van der Oord, Lucassen, Van Emmerick and EmmelKamp (2009) they evaluated the effectiveness of cognitive behavioral writing therapy (CBWT) in a group of 23 children and adolescents aged 8–18 years who experienced a range of single and recurrent traumatic experiences. CBWT uses exposure, cognitive restructuring and social sharing. These researchers conducted a pre-test and post-test to determine the efficacy of the treatments to lessen the effects of post-traumatic stress disorder (PTSD) symptoms, depressive symptoms, trauma-related cognitions and general behavioral problems. The results at post-test showed there was a significant reduction of all symptoms and this effect was maintained after six months as shown in the follow-up post-test. The mean amount of treatment sessions needed was five. This study shows short-term CBWT is a potentially effective intervention for clinically referred traumatized children.

Amaya-Jackson and DeRosa (2007) note another set of strategies many clinicians use in treating trauma in adolescents are extending the duration of selected modules beyond the normal time frame or expanding selected modules with added components. These strategies include a coping skills module with an emphasis on relaxation skills which might be expanded to include additional exercises on mindfulness to help them become more effective. As a prerequisite to facilitating trauma narration and cognitive processing a therapist may think a client would benefit from more intense auto-regulation tactics in addition to basic feelings identification and coping skills.

These researchers believe these are ways in which thoughtful application, adaptation, or augmentation of evidence based therapies can be used. Margola, Facchin, Molgora and Revenson (2010) note emotional disclosure aids in cognitive and emotional processing of trauma which provides evidence about the importance of examining paths of adjustment instead of immediate or one-shot assessment processes as well as outcomes when studying human adaptation to treatment.

Walker, et al. (2010) suggest psychologists have become increasingly concerned with the role of religion and spirituality in resolving childhood physical and sexual abuse particularly religion-related abuse. It is noted that this is a spiritual context in which a model is presented for assessing and treating religion and spirituality in trauma-focused cognitive behavior therapy. The result of this intervention in this model focuses on the client's pre-existing religious and spiritual functioning as well as changes in religion/spirituality after abuse. It is stated that this type of therapy will assist clients from various religious and spiritual affiliations to process childhood abuse. Morgan (2009) agrees the realm of spiritual healing and development may be a useful complement to emerging programs and technologies for treatment to promote healing for children and adolescents who have experienced trauma. They further state that in treating victims of child abuse trauma-focused cognitive behavior therapy has emerged as a leading treatment towards recovery of children and teens.

Silverman, et al. (2008) recognized the necessity of reviews of psychosocial treatments for reducing youth post-traumatic-stress disorder. They reported on a meta-analysis showing an effect size of .54 demonstrating reductions of the effects of child maltreatment, specifically sexual and physical abuse. A systematic review and meta-analysis conducted by Bisson and Andrew (2009) focused on psychological treatments for chronic PTSD. They found that trauma focused cognitive behavior therapy (TF-CBT) and eye movement desensitization (EMDR) were superior and recommended as first-line psychological treatments for chronic PTSD. Olff and Retsma (2007) evaluated the efficacy of brief TF-CBT for four sessions among wait-list control in 143 patients with acute PTSD with a four-month follow-up. The active treatment group had significantly fewer PTSD anxiety and depression symptoms one-week post follow-up but this difference was no longer significant after four months.

Research into pharmacological treatment of youths with PTSD is emerging but data is sorely needed specifically about maltreated youths with PTSD. Pharmacological treatment focuses on maladaptive behavioral and emotional symptoms following exposure to a stressor, especially symptoms of anxiety and depression (Kearney et al., 2009). Such treatment also focuses on the primary neurotransmitter systems involved in PTSD especially catecholamine, serotonin and gamma amino butyric acid. At the same time Stein, et al. (2009) notes several clinical guidelines which recommend that some SSRIs namely fluoxetine, paroxetine, sertraline and venlafaxine XR are appropriate as first-line treatment approaches to PTSD for adolescents. These authors conclude early indications are that second-generation antipsychotics and other agents may be useful for treatment-resistant cases and hold promise for the field.

Briere and Lanktree (2008) describe in detail the use of integrative treatment of complex trauma for adolescents providing the major treatment approaches. These include psychoeducation, distress reduction and affect regulation training, cognitive processing, titrated exposure, trigger identification and intervention, relational processing, interventions with caretakers and as well as family therapy. Details of this treatment plan can be found at JohnBriere.com website. More specific approaches include psychoeducation, hypnotherapy, grief work, affect regulation, interpersonal skills development, narrative storytelling, coping skills, stress inoculation training, school consultation and exposure-based practices, either individually or in group format. Wethington, et al. (2008) note though that cognitive-behavioral approaches in treating trauma demonstrate the best efficacy to date.

Stevens, Haynes, Ruiz and Bootzin (2007) writing about the importance of sleep in aiding recovery of adolescents from traumatic stress symptoms conclude from their implementation of several integrative, behavioral sleep intervention strategies that those with higher levels of total sleep time have reductions in traumatic stress symptoms over time. These researchers recommend the use of stimulus control, a therapy encouraging patients to attempt sleep only when they are sleepy which may be particularly helpful for adolescents with traumatic stress symptoms, sleep disturbances and substance abuse histories.

When discussing treatment of disorders in various age-groups in Jamaica, Ramkisson, Gopaul-McNichol, Davidson, Matthies, Morgan and Gibson (2008), explain that family interventions typically take the form of family therapy. They say that the models used are Salvador Minuchin's Structural Model which includes all influential family members and Murray Bowen's Transgenerational model. These researchers provide a rationale in recommending family therapy for dealing with issues relating to children and adolescents since issues can be addressed effectively within this group. Gopaul-McNicol (1997) recommends that treatment in working with immigrant families in a particular diaspora can best be understood via a comprehensive model using the multi-cultural/multimodal and multi-systems (MULTI-CMS) approach. She says the three approaches namely multi-cultural, multi-modal and multi-systems can be effectively combined in a treatment process for these persons. This writer states this approach is flexible and allows therapists to draw from different systems theories and incorporate them into an overall treatment plan. This writer stipulates that the therapist intervenes at different levels: individual, immediate and extended family, church, community and social services. Johnson, et al. (2008) note three forms of psychotherapy namely solution-focused psychotherapy by Miller, Hubble and Duncan 1996; cognitive-behavioral therapy Corey 2005; and single session psychotherapy Talmon 1990; offer promising alternatives for many patients. However, these forms of therapy are not linked precisely to treatment of specific disorders.

What are some challenges in providing evidence-based treatments to children and adolescents?

Cohen, et al. (2006) explains that most maltreated and violence exposed children either receive no treatment at all for their trauma symptoms or are treated by community therapists who typically do not provide evidence-based treatments. To begin, a close therapeutic alliance may not be forged between therapist and client or provide the foundation for treatment. This alliance would set the stage for clients to express feelings of helplessness, shame, guilt and vulnerability then focus on cathartic release of anger and develop a more positive self-image and identify meanings of traumatic events and symptoms of PTSD. Other conditions are necessary based on recommendations provided by Kearney, et al. (2009). These include attention to safety issues such as ongoing maltreatment or proximity to an abuser which must be resolved. Also they believe that youth treatments for PTSD are moderately effective since developmental considerations and multisource assessment strategies are not always taken into account. In addition, important developmental modifications must be considered for variations in language and conceptual skills, emotion regulation and coping skills, comorbidity, memory, family functioning and contextual influences.

Other factors likely to impact recovery include child and parent participation, comorbid behavior problems, length of treatment and type of family functioning.

Jaycox, et al. (2010) suggest that communities affected by disasters often face multiple challenges and child mental health resources may be particularly limited. In view of this they argue that typically affected communities do not have sufficient therapists trained in evidence-based treatments (EBT) to be able to provide each child with individual therapy. So children who receive treatment are selected based on the severity of their condition from less impaired children who receive fewer intensive services such as group therapy. Jaycox, et al. (2009) note with high incidences of trauma exposure among students, there is a need for intervention programs in schools. Nevertheless, delivery of these programs in school settings eliminates the main barriers to access to treatment. One challenge though is most programs have been designed for delivery by mental health clinicians, and only a few programs have been designed for use by non-clinicians such as school counselors and teachers.

Outcome for youths treated for PTSD is moderately effective, though developmental considerations and multisource assessment strategies are not always taken into account (Kearney et al., 2009). These researchers note that developmental modifications must be considered for variations in language and conceptual skills, emotion regulation and coping skills, comorbidity, memory, family functioning and contextual influences. They note that factors that likely impact recovery include child and parent participation, comorbid behavior problems, length of treatment and type of family functioning.

Another issue is that clinicians at the National Center for Child Traumatic Stress Center for Child and Family Health (NCTSN) focus groups note that EBT models are particularly difficult to apply to children who have neglect and abandonment histories as these children's record of trauma are often incomplete and lack a discrete event. Due to this, these narratives are hard to write. Amaya-Jackson and DeRosa (2007) found that EBT model assumptions are sometimes problematic although they assume a child can quickly learn strategies to self-regulate if the caregiver is also self-regulated. They note if caregiver's capacity and attachment issues are adequately addressed by enhanced parenting skills or alternatively a referral to therapy for themselves or the child, attending to his innermost sense of safety, the kind of remediation that will enable him to sleep peacefully through the night and help to lessen trauma in that affected child. On the contrary Sprang, Staton-Tindall and Clarke (2008) call for child welfare and mental health professionals to integrate trauma-informed assessment and treatment approaches so attempts to understand and address the complex problems endured by maltreated children can be clarified.

Fixsen, Noom, Blasé, Friedman and Wallace (2005) identified field clinician's top five reasons for not using evidence-based programs as:

The research base is not convincing

They are difficult to implement

They require too much change

They are incomplete given the problems we face and

The infrastructure for implementation does not exist or is not supported.

Although in enunciating key ingredients of therapy types, Amaya-Jackson and DeRosa (2007) report that looking across the assortment of the EBTs available, all treatment programs have utilized similar core components. These components include psychoeducation, management of anxiety and trauma reminders, trauma narration and organization, cognitive and affective processing, problem solving regarding safety and relationships, parenting skills and behavioral management addressing grief and loss, emotional regulation, hence supporting youth to resume developmental competencies that may have been delayed or lost.

These researchers state that community clinicians in accepting or challenging the use of empirically based treatment models in practice should engage in critical thinking and appraisal skills as well as monitor assessment treatment progress along the way so as to decide on intervention models to utilize. Complex child trauma histories demand a full understanding of the child's traumatic experiences. Children with multi-trauma experiences have symptom pictures influenced by multiple risk factors including the duration, dose, number, nature and subjective experience of the trauma. They explain that diagnostic considerations include but extend beyond the severity of post-traumatic stress symptoms. This is particularly true in the case of abuse and neglect with consequential attachment disruption and multiple placements. These recommendations may have emerged in part, given there are several areas addressed less frequently or in less depth in many randomized controlled treatments (RCT) to date including areas that focus on

Emotion dysregulation with feelings of intense rage and shame

Behavioral dysregulation including aggression and risk taking

Attachment issues and the impact of attachment disruption and unstable, chaotic relationships

Self-efficacy and self-perception, especially for adolescents and

Lack of purpose and meaning in life.

By extension, they suggest that youth struggling in these areas of functioning often have severe dysregulation of self systems that permeate their lives and significantly and repeatedly impact their ability to engage in treatment and achieve a sense of stability and safety. In conclusion the RCTs are hard pressed to include components addressing the difficult often time-consuming self-reflection, affective, behavioral regulation and relationship navigation skills even though a few have done so successfully.

What are some Protective Factors against Long-term Effects of Trauma on Children and Adolescents?

Vranceanu, Stevan, Hobfoll and Johnson (2007) posit that multiple forms of maltreatment in childhood including neglect, predicted decreased social support and increased stress often leads to PTSD in adulthood. The level of social support partially mediated the relationship between child maltreatment and adult PTSD symptoms, while stress fully mediated the relationship between child maltreatment and adult depression symptoms. These authors speculate that depletion of social resources over time is a determinant of poor outcomes. Schumm, Stines, Hobfoil and Jackson (2005) found that women who experienced child maltreatment were highly likely to develop PTSD but social support greatly eased the cumulative impact of these traumas. These findings underscore the importance of discovering and enhancing protective variables that may lessen the impact from child maltreatment that leads to PTSD (Kearney et al., 2009).

Kaufman (2008) posits that emerging findings strongly suggest the likelihood of a particular maltreated child developing problematic issues is influenced by both genetic and environmental factors. Yeluda and Flory (2007) note that to the extent that psychiatric illnesses result from environmental exposures, resilience may be a mediator that could explain why psychopathology does not always develop. They also explain that to the extent that biomarkers of resilience can be identified, these could be used to either predict if they are trait-related or are state-related in helping persons so afflicted to recover from traumatic events. Furthermore, if resilience is an enduring characteristic or trait that is identifiable even before trauma exposure, it could be used to predict responses to adversity in those who may be at high risk for occupational or other hazards.

The presence of a secure attachment relationship can buffer the adverse effects of trauma and provide the safety and nurturing that allows the child to process the traumatic events and return to a sense of safety and well-being. Secure attachment bonds serve as primary defenses against trauma induced psychopathology in children and even adults. Children who grow up feeling secure in their primary relationships with their care-giver(s) will undergo normal emotional development. They will be equipped to handle constructively most traumas that may occur either during childhood or later in life. According to Schore (2002) security of the attachment bond is the primary defense against trauma-induced psychopathology. On the other hand children who are subjected to disruptive separation at an early age lack this secure foundation. This disruption in a secure relationship interferes with the development of the right side of the brain which cannot be repaired later in life. This is due to the fact that neurobiological processes involved in the processing of emotion and affect regulation leading to optimal emotional development is compromised in trauma which involves the right brain and not the left brain (Solomon and Siegel, 2003). These researchers posit that few children exposed to trauma develop PTSD and few of them display PTS symptoms which can be identified through information about their age, trauma history, anxiety history and family environment. Even so, Copeland, et al. (2007) offer hope for children exposed to first life-time trauma by noting that their prognosis is generally favorable.

Gewirtz, et al. (2008) note that skills promoting healthy child development are encouragement, limit setting, monitoring, interpersonal problem solving and positive involvement. These interventions are proposed as a means in promoting effective parenting and when utilized well results in improvement in children's externalizing and internalizing problems.

CHAPTER 3 ~ A CALL TO ACTION THE TIME IS NOW

Trauma is defined as the expressed threat or witnessing of physical harm and the associated emotional feelings. It is believed that exposure to various forms of trauma appear relatively common during childhood and adolescence. In effect, psychological and physical development of youths can be severely handicapped by various forms of abuse. The younger the child when faced with maltreatment and exposure to traumatic incidences, the greater the impact. Earlier abuse though affects children in ways which results in dysregulation of the HPA axis that can lead to major brain system dysfunctions which sometimes results in them being impacted by PTSD or CPTSD depending on the degree of trauma they sustained in earlier years.

It is known that stress at extreme levels can negatively impact brain development. In particular, the hippocampus is damaged by stress and results in poor functioning of the brain including memory function. The impact may be so great that intense trauma in the early years result in unhealthy responses and even death in adulthood. Frontal lobe abnormalities in pediatric PTSD are related to physical abuse and are predictors of psychiatric illnesses later in life including mood disorders. Childhood sexual abuse is associated with various psychopathologies including depression, substance abuse, personality disorders, PTSD and anxiety disorders in adulthood.

Various instruments are available to help with the assessment of both children and adolescents although in some parts of the world, psychological testing is expensive and may not even be standardized on the young population. Therapists too may not be able to access training in evidence-based treatments suitable for their population of children and adolescents.

In conclusion, disorders in children must be carefully assessed by taking a detailed trauma history about the onset of abuse, taking into consideration physical and emotional symptoms to enable correct diagnosis and treatment. Symptoms of PTSD differ substantially between children and adolescents while some instruments used for assessment span a number of developmental stages.

To prevent the compromising of diagnoses, both child and parent report measures should be used in assessment. Other instruments provide a normative adjustment for 17 year olds. Trauma focused cognitive behavior therapy (TF-CBT) is the only well-established psychosocial treatment available for children who are impacted by trauma, whereas cognitive behavioral insight oriented therapies are the most developed and researched approach for treatment of PTSD (Solomon and Johnson, 2002). However, Complex PTSD (CPTSD) or disorders of extreme stress are extremely difficult to treat. Nevertheless, a few pharmacological treatments are available for older children and adolescents.

Noteworthy too is most maltreated and traumatized children and adolescents receive no treatment. Sometimes developmental concerns and multi-score assessments are not used in the assessment and diagnosis. However, resources are often few in some communities facing disasters. Also, there are insufficient numbers of adequately trained therapists to deliver services. Consider too that an adequate support system for youths may be unavailable to sustain the length of treatment required for best client care. A key point to note is both genetic and environmental factors can serve as protective agencies for youth in allaying development of disorders. An essential consideration is that secure attachment with care-giver(s) can also protect children and adolescents from the full impact of trauma.

Conclusions

Many children and adolescents in various parts of the world are traumatized and suffer from various disorders including post-traumatic stress disorder and complex post-traumatic stress disorder. They are in need of assessment, accurate diagnoses and treatment. Nevertheless, members of this youthful population are often unable to access psychological testing and receive accurate diagnosis. When testing is available it may be too expensive and may not even be standardized on the population that is in need of bio-psychosocial care, hence assessments may need to be adapted. It is also true that many therapists may not be able to access training in administering, scoring and interpreting tests to help them in making accurate diagnoses. Training of therapists in administering evidence based therapies such as TF-CBT and CBT may not be available in their country either. As a result, many children and adolescents in need of care are not able to access suitable effective therapies. A vital consideration is that research findings reveal some victims of trauma possess protective factors which stave off the worst consequences of maltreatment.

Discussion

The conclusions drawn from this research have implications for practice. There is a need to take into consideration the culture that exists in developing nations such as Jamaica to enact meaningful changes. For too long have parents and teachers been struggling with children who are traumatized by various incidences in this society and yearning to gain access to effective bio-psychosocial care. As shown earlier, Wright bemoans the lack of provision of appropriate services for the young population in this country. It is my belief that many of our clinicians are not trained in providing evidence-based therapies for Jamaicans with various disorders linked to traumatic occurrences.

One of the oldest established universities in the Caribbean region has had difficulties sustaining the offering of masters and doctoral level courses in clinical psychology to students over many years. Obtaining practicum placements is also a major challenge for most clinicians here, since spaces providing such opportunities are extremely limited. An important point to note is that most schools and colleges are not equipped with resources and facilities for assessment, diagnostic and treatment services that could benefit traumatized students. As a result, the society is faced with mentally and emotionally disturbed young persons who sometimes commit serious crimes and end up in jails or sometimes on the street. It is time that Jamaican psychologists and other professionals take note of the inadequate services available to our children and adolescents and hasten to involve all stake-holders in making the needed changes. The journey begins with the will to make meaningful adjustments.

Future Research

Future research could be done by including voices of educational, counseling and clinical psychologists who work in both private and public sector organizations so as to fully understand the work in which they engage as it relates to children, adolescents and their families in Jamaica. No longer should territorial lines be drawn between these groups of professionals. If we view the lives of families and their young to be of significance, it requires the forging of partnerships between all stake-holders to meaningfully enact needed changes in this country.

References

Ahmad, A. Larsson, B. & Sundelin-Wahlstein, V. (2007). EMDR treatment for children with PTSD: Results of a randomized controlled trial. Nordic Journal of Psychiatry, 61, 349–354.

Ahrens, J. & Rexford, L. Cognitive Processing Therapy for Incarcerated Adolescents with PTSD. In Trauma and Juvenile Delinquency Theory Research and Interventions pp. 201–216 (2002). Greenwalded http://www.ncjirs.gov/app/publications/abstract aspx?1D=198442

Amaya-Jackson, L. & DeRosa, R.R. Treatment Consideration for Clinicians in Applying Evidence-Based Practice to Complex Presentations in Child Trauma. In Journal Traumatic Stress, Vol. 20, No. 4, August 2007, pp. 379–390 (C _ 2007).

American Psychiatric Association (2000). Diagnostic and statistical manual of mental disorders (text revision) (4th ed.). Washington, DC: American Psychiatric Association.

American Psychological Association Committee on Professional Practice and Standards. Guidelines for psychological evaluations in child protection matters (1998).

American Psychological Association Committee on Professional Practice www.apa.org.1988.

Amir, N. Coles, M.E., & Foa, E.B. Automatic and Strategic Activation and Inhibition of the Threat Relevant Information in Post-traumatic Stress Disorder. Cognitive Therapy and Research Vol. 26, no. 2, Oct. 2002, pp. 645–655.

Anda, R.F., Croft, J.B. Felliti, V.J., Nordenburg, D. Giles, W.H. Williamson, D.F. & Giovino, G.A. Adverse Childhood Experiences and Smoking during Adolescence and Adult-hood. JAMA, Nov. 3, 1999–Vol 282, No.17. American Medical Association.

Avinger, K. A., & Jones, R. A. (2007). Group treatment of sexually abused adolescent girls: A review of outcome studies. American Journal of Family Therapy, 35, 315–326.

Bandura, A. (1977). Social learning theory. Englewood Cliffs, N.J.: Prentice- Hall.

Bartley-Small, M. How Socio-economic Status. Exposure to Violence and Family Structure Influence Depressive Symptoms in Children. International Journal of Arts & Sciences 3 (8) 302-319 (2010). International Journal.org

Beck, A. T. (1976). Cognitive therapy and the emotional disorders. International University Press.

Beers, S.R., & DeBellis, M.D. Neuropsychological Function in Children With Maltreatment-Related Posttraumatic Stress Disorder. Am. J. Psychiatry 159:483–486, March 2002 American Psychiatric Association.

Bendall, S., Jackson, H.J., Hulbert C.A., & McGory, P.D. (2008). Childhood Trauma and Psychotic Disorder: a Systematic Critical Review of the Evidence. Schizophrenia Bulletin, Oxford Journals, Vol. 34, Issue 3, pp. 568–579.

Bisson, J., & Andrew, M. Psychological treatment of post-traumatic stress disorder (PTSD). The Chocrane Library, Depression, Anxiety and Neurosis Group. Published online: Jan. 21, 2009.

Bratton, S. C., Ray, D. Rhine, T., & Jones, L. (2005). The efficacy of play therapy with children: A Meta-Analytic review of treatment outcomes. Professional Psychology: Research and Practice, 36 (4), 376–90.

Briere, J. & Lanktree, C. Integrative Treatment of Complex Trauma for Children (ITCT-C). A Guide for the Treatment of Multiply-Traumatized Children Aged Eight to Twelve Years MCAVIC-USC Child and Adolescent Trauma Program National Child Traumatic Stress Network 2008.http://www.johnbriere.com/

Briere, J. & Scott, C. (1996). Trauma Symptom Checklist for Children (TSCC) Professional Manual. Odessa, Fl: Psychological Assessment Resources.

Briere, J. & Scott, C. (2006). Principles of Trauma Therapy: A Guide to Symptoms, Evaluation and Treatment. books.google.com.Sage Pub.Inc.

Bruce, J., Fisher, P.A., Pears, K.C., & Levine, S. (2009). Morning Cortisol Levels in Preschool-Aged Foster Children: Differential Effects of Maltreatment Type. Dev. Psychobiology 2009, January; 51 (1): 14–23.

Caffo, E. & Belaise, C. (2007). In The Mental Health of Children and Adolescents an Area of Global Neglect ed. Remschmidt, H., Nurcombe, B., Belfer, M.L., Sartorus, N. A report from: World Psychiatric Association. Presidential Program on Child Mental Health. http://google.com.

Carey, P. (2008). The Effect of Trauma and Violence on Children and Adolescents http://www.sahealthinfo.org.

Carew, S.A. Transportability of Trauma-Focused Cognitive Behavior Therapy: A Case Study with Adolescents in a Residential Treatment Setting. Philadelphia College of Osteopathic Medicine DigitalCommons@PCOM Psychology Dissertations Student Dissertations, Theses and Papers 2007.

Caribbean Child Development Centre, U.W.I Mona (2005). Documentation of Interpersonal Violence Prevention Programmes for Children in Jamaica. Prepared for UNICEF, Jamaica.

Carrion, V.G., Weems, C.F., Watson, C., Eliez, S., Menon, V., & Reiss, A.L. Psychiatry Research 2009 June 30; 172(3): 226–234.

Carpenter, L. L., Carvalho, J. P., Tyrka, A. R., Wier, L. M., Mello, A. F., & Mello, M. F. et al. (2007). Decreased Adrenocorticotropic Hormone and Cortisol Responses to Stress in Healthy Adults Reporting Significant Childhood Maltreatment. Biological Psychiatry, 62, 1080–1087.

Carter-Visscher, R. M., Naugle, A. E., Bell, K. M., & Suvak, M. K. (2007). Ethics of asking trauma-related questions and exposing participants to arousal-inducing stimuli. Journal of Trauma & Dissociation, 8, 27–55.

Cicchetti, D. Toth, S.L.Child Maltreatment. In Annual Review of Clinical Psychology 2005 1, Proquest Central.

Classen, C.C., Cavanaugh, C.E., Kaupp, J.W., Aggarwal, R. Palesh, O.G., Koopman, C., Kraemer, H.C., & Spiegel, D. A Comparison of Trauma Focused and Present Focused Group Therapy for Survivors of Childhood Sexual Abuse: A Randomized Controlled Trial: American Psychological Association. Psychological Trauma: Theory, Research, Practice and Policy 2011 Vol. 3, No.1, 84–93.

Cohen, J.A., & Mannarino, A.P. Trauma-Focused Cognitive Behavioral Therapy for Children and Parents. In Child and Adolescents Mental vol. 13, Issue 4, pp. 158–162. Nov. 2008.

Cohen, J.A., Mannarino, A.P., Murray, L.K., & Ingleman, R. (2006). Psychosocial Interventions for Maltreated and Violence-Exposed Children. The Society for the Psychological Study of Social Issues.

Cohen, J.A., Belinger, E., Mannarino, A.P. & Steer, R. A. Multi-site Randomized Controlled Trial for Children with Abuse-Related PTSD Symptoms. Journal American Child Adolescent Psychiatry 2004 April 43 (4): 393-402.

Cohen, J.A., & Mannarino, A.P. Treatment of Childhood Traumatic Grief. Journal of Clinical Child and Adolescent Psychiatry. 2004, vol. 33, no.4 819–831. Lawrence Erlburn Ass. Inc.

Cohen, J. A., & Mannarino, A. P. (1996). A treatment outcome study for sexually abused preschool children: Initial findings. Journal of the American Academy of Child & Adolescent Psychiatry, 35, 42–50.

Collin-Vezina, D., & Herbert, M. Comparing Dissociation and PTSD in Sexually Abused School-Aged Girls. The Journal of Nervous and Mental Disease Vol. 193, No.1, Jan. 2005.

Cook, A., Spinazzola J., Ford J., Lanktree C., Blaustein, M., Cloitre, M., DeRosa, R., Hubbard, R., Kagan R., Liautaud, J., Mallah, K., Olafson, E., & vander kolk, B. Complex Trauma in Children and Adolescents. Psychiatric Annals, May 2005, 35, 5, ProQuest Central.

Copeland, W.E., Keeper, G., Angold, A., & Costello, J.E. Integrative Treatment of Complex Trauma for Adolescents (ITCT-A). A Guide for the Treatment of Multiply-Traumatized Youth. ARCH GEN PSYCHIATRY Vol 64, May 2007.

Courtois, C.A. Complex Trauma, Complex Reactions. Assessment and Treatment. Psychological Trauma: Theory Research, Practice and Policy, 2008, Vol. S., No. 1 86–100. American Psychological Association.

Courtois, C. A. Complex Trauma, Complex Reactions. Assessment and Treatment. Psychotherapy: Theory, Research, Practice, Training 2004. Vol.41, No.4 412-425.

Crawford-Brown, C. The Impact of Parenting on Conduct Disorder in Jamaican Male Adolescents. Summer (1999) 34, 134 p.14.Proquest Psychological Journals.

Creswell, J.W. (1998). Qualitative Inquiry and Research Design. Choosing Among Five Traditions. Sage Pub. New York.

Dalglieish, T. Meiser- Stedman R., Kassam-Adams, N., Ehlers A., Winston, E., Smith P. Bryant, B. Mayou R.A., & Yule W. Predictive Validity of Acute Stress Disorder in Children and Adolescents. The British Journal of Psychiatry (2008).

Dalgleish, T., Meiser-Stedman R., & Smith, P. Cognitive Aspects of Post-traumatic Stress Reactions and their Treatment in Children and Adolescents: An Empirical Review and Some Recommendations. Behavioral and Cognitive Psychotherapy, 2005; 33.

Debellis, M.D. The Psychobiology of Neglect. Child Maltreatment, vol.10. No.2 pp. 150–172.May 2005 http://cmx.sagepub.com/content10/2/150.

Diehl, A.S. & Prout, M.F. Effects of Posttraumatic Stress Disorder and Child Sexual Abuse on Self-efficacy Development. American Journal of Orthopsychiatry, 2002 vol. 72, No. 2, 262–265.

Documentation of Interpersonal Violence Prevention Programs for Children in Jamaica. Prepared for UNICEF Jamaica. Caribbean Child Development Centre. School of Continuing Studies, U.W.I (2005).

Dubowitz, H. & Bennett, S. Physical Abuse and Neglect of Children. Lancet 2007; 369:1891–99.

Edwards, D.J. (2005). Evaluation of a Behavioral Scale Designed to Address Adolescent Conduct Disorder in Jamaica. Temple University. ProQuest Dissertations and Theses, (UMI no. 3176824).

Egeland, B. (2009). Attachment-Based Intervention and Prevention Program for Young Children. In Encyclopedia on Early Childhood Development. http://www.child-encyclopedia.com

Feather, J.C., & Ronan, R. Trauma-Focused Cognitive Behavior Therapy for Abused Children with Post-Traumatic Stress Disorder: A Pilot Study. New Zealand Journal of Psychology: November 2006; 35.

Ferrari, A.M. The impact of Culture upon Child-Rearing Practices and Definitions of Maltreatment. Child Abuse and Neglect 26, (2002) pp. 793–813.

First, M.B., Frances, A., & Pincus, H.A. DSM-IV-TR (2002). Handbook of Differential Diagnosis. American Psychiatric Publishing, Inc.

Fixsen, D. L., Naoom, S. F., Blase, K. A., Friedman, R. M. & Wallace, F. (2005). Implementation Research: A Synthesis of the Literature. Tampa, FL: University of South Florida, Louis de la Parte Florida Mental Health Institute, The National Implementation Research Network (FMHI Publication #231).

Foa, E.B., Ehlers A., Clark, D.M., Tolin, D.F., & Orsillo, S.M. The Posttraumatic Cognitions Inventory (PTCI). Development of Validation. Psychological Assessment 1999, Vol.11, 3, 303–314.

Ford, J.D. (2005). Treatment Implications of Alterations of Altered Effect Regulation and Information Processing following Child Maltreatment: Psychiatric Annals 35, 410–419.

Gewirtz, A., Forgatch, M., & Wieling E. Parenting Practices as Potential Mechanisms for Child Adjustment following Mass Trauma. Journal of Marital and Family Therapy. Ap. 2008, Vol. 34, No.2 pp. 177–192.

Goldfinch, M. (2009). Putting Humpty Together Again: Working With Parents to Help Children Who Have Experienced Early Trauma. The Australian and New Zealand Journal of Family Therapy 2009 pp. 284–299.

Gopaul-McNichol, S.A. (1997). A Multi-cultural Multi-modal Multi-systems Approach to Working with Immigrant Families: A New Paradigm. Praeger Pub., Greenwood Pub. Group Inc.

Halligan, S.L., Michael, T., Clark, D.M., & Ehlers, A. Post-traumatic Stress Disorder Following Assault. The Role of Cognitive Processing, Trauma Memory and Appraisals. Journal of Consulting and Clinical Psychology 2003 vol. 71, No. 3, 419–431.

Handwerger, K. (2009). Differential Patterns of HPA Activity and Reactivity in Adult Posttraumatic Stress Disorder and Major Depressive Disorder. Harvard Review Psychiatry vol. 17, No. 3.

Harris, W.W., Lieberman, A.F., & Marans, S. In the best interests of society. Journal of Child Psychology and Psychiatry 48: 3 /4 (2007).

Haugaard, J.J. (2004b). Recognizing and treating uncommon behavioral and emotional disorders in children and adolescents who have been severely maltreated: Dissociative disorders. Child Maltreatment, 9, 146–153.

Haugaard, J.J. & Hazan, C.(2003). Adoption as a Natural Experiment. Development of Psychopathology, vol. 15/Issue04/Dec. pp.909-926.

Heflin, A. H., & Deblinger, E. (2006). Treatment of a Sexually Abused Adolescent with Posttraumatic Stress Disorder. In M. A. Reinecke, F. M. Dattilio, & A. Freeman (Eds.), Cognitive Therapy with Children and Adolescents: A Casebook for Clinical Practice (2nd ed., pp. 214–246). New York: Guilford.

Heim, C., & Nemeroff, C.B. Neurobiology of Posttraumatic Stress Disorder. CNS Spectr. January 2009; 14:1 (Suppl. (1): 13-24.

Herman, J.L. Complex PTSD. A Syndrome in Survivors of Prolonged and Repeated Trauma. Journal of Traumatic Stress, vol. 5, No. 5, No. 3, 1992(a).

Hickling, F.W. (1994). Violence in Jamaica. Caribbean Journal of Religious Studies,15, 3-13.

Hirai, M., & Clum, G.A. (2005). An internet-based self-change program for traumatic event related fear, distress, and maladaptive coping. Journal of Traumatic Stress, 18(6), 631–636.

Holdbrook, T.Z., & Hoyt, D.B. J. Trauma (2004), Feb. 56 (2) 284-290. Pub Med PMID 14960969.

http://www.dcoalition.org

http://www.indigenousportal.com

http://www.pioj.gov.jm

http://www.who.int/mental_health/Jamaica_who

Hullette, A., Freyd, J.J., Pears, K.C., Kim, H.K, Fisher P.A., Baker & Blease, K.A. Disassociation and Posttraumatic Symptoms in Maltreated Pre-School Children. In Journal of Child and Adolescent Trauma, 1: 93–108, 2008.

Huppert, J.D., Foa, E.B., McNally, R.J., & Cahill, S.P. (2011). Stress-Induced and Fear Circuitry Disorders. Ed. edited by Gavin Andrews, M.D., Dennis S. Charney, Paul J. Sirovatka, M.S. http://www.appi.org/SiteCollection Documents.

Jamaica Child Development Centre, School of Continuing Studies, Mona, (2005). Documentation of Interpersonal Violence Prevention Programmes for Children in Jamaica. Prepared for UNICEF-Child Development Centre.

Jaycox, L.H., Cohen, J.A. Mannarino, A.P., Walker, D.W., Langley, A.K, Gegenheimer, K.L., Scott, M., & Schonlau M. Children's Mental Health Care following Hurricane Katrina: A Field Trial of Trauma-Focused Psychotherapies. Journal of Trauma Stress (2010), April 23 (2), 223–231.

Jaycox, L.H., Langley, A. K., Stein, B.D., Wong, M., Sharma, P., Scott, M., & Schonlau, M. Support for Students exposed to Trauma. School of Mental Health. June 1, 2009. http://www.ncbi.nlm.nih.gov//PMC/articles/PMC29.

Johnson, R., & Coley, T. (2008). Psychological Assessment. In Perspectives in Caribbean Psychology, Hickling, F.W., Matthies, B.K., Morgan K., Gibson, R.C. Eds. (pp. 630-651).CAIMENSA, University of the West Indies, Mona.

Johnson, R., Weller, P., Williams-Brown, S., & Pottinger, A. (2008). The Application of Traditional Psychotherapy Models in the Caribbean. In Perspectives in Caribbean Psychology, Hickling, F.W., Matthies, B.K., Morgan, K., Gibson, R.C. Eds. (pp. 537-557). CAIMENSA, University of the West Indies, Mona.

Kaplow, J.B., & Widom, C.S. Age of Onset of Child Maltreatment Predicts Long-Term Mental Health Outcome. Journal of Abnormal Psychology 2007, vol. 116, No.1, 176–187.

Kaufman, J. Genetic and Environmental Modifiers of Risk and Resiliency in Maltreated Children. In Developmental Psychopathology and Wellness, Genetic and Environmental Modifiers of Risk and Resiliency in Maltreated Children (2008). Washington D.C. APA.

Kaufman, J., Yang, B., Palumberi, D., Housheryar, S., Lipschitzn, D., Krystal, J.H., & Geleruter, J. Ed. (2004). McEwen, B.S. The Rockefeller University, New York, N.Y.

Kaufman, J., & Charney, D. Effects of early stress on brain structure and function. Implications for Understanding the Relationship between Child Maltreatment and Depression. Development and Psychopathology (2001), 13:pp. 451-471.

Kearney, C.A., Wechsler, A. Kaur, H., & Lemos-Miller, A.M. (2009). Posttraumatic Stress Disorder in Maltreated Youth: A Review of Contemporary Research and Thought. Clinical Child Family Psychology Review (2010) 13:46–76 DOI 10.1007/s10567-009-0061-4.

Keeton, C.P., & Ginsberg, G.S. Combining and Sequencing Medication and Cognitive Behavior Therapy for Childhood Anxiety Disorders. International Review of Psychiatry, April 2008, 20 (2). pp. 159–164.

Khouri, L. Tang, Y.L., Bradley B., Cabells, J.F., & Ressler, K.J. Substance Abuse, Childhood Traumatic Experience and Post-Traumatic Stress Disorder in an urban civilian population. Depression Anxiety 2010, Dec. 27, (12): 1077-86www.ncbi.nlm.nih.gov

Koverola, C., Murtaugh, C. A., Connors, K. M., Reeves, G., & Papas, M. A. (2007). Children exposed to intra-familial violence: Predictors of attrition and retention in treatment. Journal of Aggression, Maltreatment, and Trauma, 14, 19–42.

Lanktree, C.B., Gilbert, A.M., Briere, J., Taylor, N., Chen, K., Maida, C.A, & Saltzman, W.R. (2008). Multi-informant Assessment of Maltreated Children: Convergent and Discriminant Validity of the TSCC and TSCYC. (2007). Child Abuse and Neglect 32 (2008) 621–625.

Larkin, W., & Read, J. Childhood Trauma and Psychosis: Evidence Pathways and Implications. Journal of Postgraduate Medicine. Vol. 2008, Vol. 54 Issue 4. pp. 287–293.

Laugharne, J., Lilee, A., & Janca, A. Role of Psychological Trauma in the Cause and Treatment of Anxiety and Depressive Disorders. Current Opinion in Psychiatry 2010, 23:25–29.

Lawson, D.M. Understanding and Treating Children who Experience Interpersonal Maltreatment: Empirical Findings. Journal of Counseling and Development. JCD Spring 2009, 87, 2. ProQuest Central 204.

Lemos-Miller, A.M. The effects of trauma experiences in maltreated adolescents with respect to Familial and Cultural Variables Ph.D Thesis, University of Nevada, 2008.

Lieberman, A.F., Vanhorn, P., & Ippen, C.G. Toward Evidence-Based Treatment: Child-Parent Psychotherapy with Pre-schoolers Exposed to Marital Violence. In Journal of American Academic Child Adolescent Psychiatry, Dec. 2005, 44:12 72-79.

Margola, D., Facchin, F., Molgora, S., & Revenson, T.O. Cognitive and Emotional Processing Through Writing Among Adolescents who Experienced the Death of a Classmate. American Psychological Association. Psychological Trauma: Theory, Research, Practice and Policy 2010, Vol. 2, No.3, 250-260.

Margolin, G., & Vickerman, K.A. Post-traumatic Stress in Children and Adolescents Exposed to Family Violence: Overview and Issues. Published in final edited form as: 2007 December 1; 38(6): 613–619.10.1037/0735-7028.38.6.613.

Markese, S. Taping Together Broken Bones. Treatment of the Trauma of Infant Physical and Sexual Abuse. J. of Infant Child, and Adolescent Psychotherapy 6 (4): 309-326, Fall 2007.

Mathews, C.A., Nirmaljit, K., & Stein, M.B. Depression & Anxiety 25: Issue 9 (2008). pp. 742–751 http://www. mendeley.com/share.

McIntosh, S., & Mata, M. (2008). Posttraumatic Stress Disorder in Children. Early Detection Posttraumatic Stress Disorder in Children. Journal of Trauma, Nursing Career and Technical Education.

Meeks-Gardener, J. Powell, C.A., Thomas, J.A. & Millard, D. (2003). Perceptions and Experiences of Violence among Secondary School Students in Urban Jamaica. Pan American Journal of Public Health 14, (2),97–103.

Meiser-Stedman, R., Smith, P., Bryan,T. R. Salmon, K.,Yule, W., Dalgeish, & T., Nixon, R.D.V. Journal of Child Psychology & Psychiatry. 50:4 (2009). pp. 432–430.

Meiser-Stedman, R., Smith, P., Gluckman, E., & Yule, W. Parent and Child Agreement for Acute Stress Disorder and other Psychopathology in a Prospective Study of Children and Adolescents Exposed to Single-Event Trauma. Journal of Abnormal Psychology (2007) 35: 191–201.

Morgan, O.J. (2009). Journal of Addictions & Offender Counseling October 2009, Volume 30.

Moroz, K.J. (2005). The Effects of Psychological Children and Trauma in Adolescents. http://mentalhealth.vermont.gov.

Mueser, K.T., & Taub, J. Trauma and PTSD Among Adolescents With Severe Emotional Disorders Involved in Multiple Service Systems. PSYCHIATRIC SERVICES psychiatryonline.org June 2008, Vol. 59 No. 6, 633.

Nader, K. Culture and Assessment of Trauma in Youths. In Cross Cultural Assessment of Psychological Trauma in Youths. International and Cultural Psychology 2007, Part 2, pp. 169–196.

O'Donnell, D.A., Joshi, P.T., & Lewin, S.M. Training in Developmental Responses to Trauma for Child Service Providers. Psychiatryonline.org January 2007. Vol. 58, No.1.

Olff, S.M., & Retsma, J.B. Treatment of Acute Post-traumatic Stress Disorder with Brief Cognitive-Therapy: A Randomized Controlled Trial. American Journal of Psychiatry 2007: 164: 82.

Pelcovitz, D., Van der Kolk B., Roth S. Mandel, F., Kaplan, S. & Resick, P. Development of a Criteria Set and a Structured Interview for Disorders of Extreme Stress (SIDES). Journal of Traumatic Stress, Vol. 10, No. 1, 1997.

Perry, B.D. (2009). Examining Child Maltreatment through a Neurodevelopment Lens: Clinical Application of the Neurosequential Model of Therapeutics. Journal of Loss and Trauma 14: 240–255.

Putman, F.W. The Impact of Trauma on Child Development. Juvenile and Family Court. Journal vol.57 no.1, National Council of Juvenile and Family Court Judges.Winter 2006: 1–11.

Putman, F.W. Ten-year Research Update Review: Child Sexual Abuse. Journal American Academy Child Adolescent Psychiatry 2003, 42 (3) 269–278.

Ramkisson, M., Gopaul-McNicol, S., Davidson, B., Matthies, B. K., & Brown- Earle, O. (2008). Family Life in the Caribbean Assessment and Counseling Models. In

Perspectives in Caribbean Psychology eds. Hickling, F.W., Matthies B.K., Morgan, K., Gibson R. C. CAIMENSA, University of the West Indies, Mona.

Ramos, S., & Boyle, G.J. Ritual and Medical Circumcision among Filipino Boys: Evidence of Post-Traumatic Stress Disorder (2000). Humanities and Social Sciences papers. http://epublications.bond.edu.an/hss_pubs/114.

Rivard, J.C., Bloom, S.L., McCorkle, D., & Abramovitz, R. (2005). Preliminary results of a study examining the implementation and effects of a trauma recovery framework for youths in residential treatment. Therapeutic Community: The International Journal for Therapeutic and Supportive Organizations 26(1): 83–96.

Ross, G., & O'Carroll, P. (2004). Cognitive behavioral psychotherapy intervention in childhood sexual abuse: Identifying new directions from the literature. Child Abuse Review, 13, 51–64.

Rossman, B. B., R., & Ho, J. (2000). Posttraumatic Response and Children Exposed to Parental Violence. Journal of Aggression, Maltreatment, and Trauma, 3, 85–106.

Saigh, P.A. (2004). Mental Measurements Yearbook with Tests in Print. Test Name: Children's PTSD Inventory. A Structured Interview for Diagnosing Post-Traumatic Stress Disorder.

Samms-Vaughn, M.E., Jackson, M., & Ashley, D. E. (2005). Urban Jamaican Children's Exposure to Community Violence. West Indian Medical Journal; 54 (1), 14–25.

Saunders, B.E. Understanding Children Exposed to Violence. Toward an Integration of Overlapping Fields. Journal of Interpersonal Violence, vo. 18, no. 4, April 2003 pp. 356–376.

Schore, A.N. Dysregulation of the Right Brain: A Fundamental Mechanism of Traumatic Attachment and the Psychopathogenesis of Post-Traumatic Stress Disorder. Australian and New Zealand Journal of Psychiatry 2002, 36, 9–30.

Schumm, J.A. Stines, R., Hobfoil, S.E., & Jackson, A.P. The Double-Barreled Burden of Child Abuse and Current Stressful Circumstances on Adult Women: The Kindling Effect of Early Traumatic Experience. Journal of Trauma Stress. 2005, Oct. 18 (5) 467–76.

Schwartz, E.D., & Perry, B.D. The Post-traumatic response in children and adolescents. Psychiatric Clinics of North America. 17 (2): 311–326, 1994.

Sheinberg, M., & True, F. Treating Family Relational Trauma: A Recursive Process Using a Decision Dialogue. Family Process; June 2008; 47, 2: ProQuest Central p.173.

Shevlin, M., Dorahy, M.J., & Adamson, G. Trauma and Psychosis: An Analysis of the National Comorbidity Survey. American Journal Psychiatry 164:1January (2007). ajp.psychiatryonline.org

Shetty, G. (2011, May 29). Under diagnosed and Untreated. Alarming Number of Children are Classified Mentally ill. The Sunday Gleaner p.A4.

Silverman, W.R., Ortiz, C.D., Viswesvaran, C. Burns, B.J., Kolko, D.J., Putnam, F.W., & Amaya-Jackson, L. Evidence-Based Psychosocial Treatments for Children and Adolescents Exposed to Traumatic Events. Journal of Clinical Child & Adolescent Psychology, 37(1),156–183, 2008. Copyright # Taylor & Francis Group, LLC ISSN: 1537-4416 print=1537-4424 online DOI: 10.1080/15374410701818293.

Silverman, W.K. (1994). Structured diagnostic interviews. In: International Handbook of Phobic and Anxiety Disorders in Children and Adolescents: Issues in Clinical Child Psychology, Ollendick TH, King NJ, eds. New York: Plenum, pp 293–315.

Smith, P., Bryant R., Salmon, K., Yule W., Dalgeish, T., & Nixon R.D.V. Journal of Child Psychology & Psychiatry. 50:4 (2009) pp. 432-440. Blackwell Pub. www.mendely.com.

Smith, P., Yule, W., Perrin, S., Tranah, T., Dalgleish, T., & Clarke, D.M. Cognitive-Behavioral Therapy for PTSD in Children and Adolescents: A Preliminary Randomized Controlled Trial. Journal Academic Child Adolescence. Psychiatry 2007:46 (8): 1050–1061.

Solomon, M.F., & Siegel, D.J. (2003). Healing Trauma Attachment, Trauma, The Brain and the Mind. pp. 221–281. N.Y. Norton.

Solomon, S.D. & Johnson, D.M. Psychotherapy in Practice, vol. 58 (8), 947–95 (2002). Wiley Interscience.wiley.com.

Sprang, G., Staton-Tindall, M. & Clark, J. Trauma Exposure and the Drug Endangered Child Center for the Study of Violence Against Children, University of Kentucky, Lexington, KY Journal of Traumatic Stress, Vol. 21, No.3, June (2008), pp. 333–339.

Stein, D.J., Ipser, J., & McAnda, N. Pharmacotherapy of Post-traumatic Stress Disorder: A Review of Meta-Analyses and Treatment Guidelines. CNS Spectrum 2009, Jan. 14 (I supp.I): 25–31.

Stevens, S., Haynes, P.L., Ruiz, B., & Bootzin, R.R. Effects of Behavior Sleep Medicine. Intervention on Trauma Symptoms in Adolescents recently treated for Substance Abuse. In Substance Abuse. Vol. 28, Issue (2) 2007 p. 21–23.

Stirling, J. & Amaya-Jackson, L. Understanding the Behavioral and Emotional Consequences of Child Abuse. American Academy of Pediatrics. Vol. 122, No.3, Sept 1, 2008. pp. 667–673.

Tarullo, A.R. & Gunmar, M.R. Child Maltreatment and Developing HPA Axis. Hormones and Behavior (2006). www.Sciencedirect.com.

The National Child Traumatic Stress Network (2011). www.nctsn.org.

The Sunday Gleaner of April 24, 2011 www.jamaica-gleaner.com.

The Sunday Gleaner of May 29, 2011. www.jamaica-gleaner.com.

Thompson, K. M., Crosby, R. D., Wonderlich, S. A., Mitchell, J.C.,Redline, J., Demuth, G., Smith & Hoseltine, B. (2003). Psychopathology and sexual trauma in childhood and adulthood. Journal of Traumatic Stress, 16, 35–38.Vol.16, No.1, Feb.2003, pp. 35–38.

Topham, G. L., Wampler, K.S., Gayatri, T., & Rolling, E. Predicting Parent and Child Outcomes of a Filial Therapy Program International Journal of Play Therapy (2011). Association for Play Therapy 2011, Vol. 20, No. 2, 79–93.

Tortello, R. Jamaica Gleaner: Pieces of the Past: The Jews in Jamaica. August 4, 2003. Jamaica gleaner.com.

Tufnell, G. (2005). Eye movement desensitization and reprocessing in the treatment of pre-adolescent children with post-traumatic symptoms. Clinical Child Psychology and Psychiatry, 10, 587–600.

Van der Kolk, B.A., Pynoos, R.S., Cicchetti, D., Maylee, C., D'Andrea, W., Putnam, F.W., Stolbach, C.B, Cloitre, M., Liberman, A. F., Glenn, S., Sinzzala, J., & Teicher, M. Proposal to include a Developmental Trauma Disorder Diagnosis for Children & Adolescents in DSM-V Feb.1, 2009. http://www.citeserv.ist.psu.edu/viewdoc/downloaddoi10.11.1685644&rep1&typepdf

Van der Kolk, B.A. (2005). Developmental Trauma Disorder: Towards a Rational Diagnosis for Children with Complex Trauma Histories. http://www.hogg.utexas.edu/uploads/documents/dev_trauma_disorder.pdf

Van der Oord, S. Lucassen, S. Van Emmerik, A.A. & Emmel Kamp, P.M. (2009). Treatment of Post-traumatic Stress Disorder in Children using Cognitive Behavioral Writing Therapy. Clinical Psychology Psychotherapy 17, 240-247. John Wiley and Sons.

Van der Vegt, E. J. M., Van der Ende, J., Kirschbaum, C., Verhulst, F.C., & Tiemeier, H. (2009). Early Neglect and Abuse Predict Diurnal Cortisol Patterns in Adults: A Study of International Adoptees. Psychoneuroendocrinology, 34, 660–669.

Van Voorhees, E., & Scarpa, A. (2004). The effects of child maltreatment on the hypothalamic-pituitary-adrenal axis. Trauma, Violence, and Abuse, 5, 333–352.

Veltman, M. W. M., & Browne, K. D. (2001). Three Decades of Child Maltreatment Research: Implications of the School Years. Trauma, Violence, and Abuse, 2, 215–239.

Vranceanu, A., Hobfoll, S.E., & Johnson, R.J. Child Multi-Type Maltreatment and Associated Depression and PTSD symptoms: The Role of Social Support and Stress. Child Abuse Neglect 2007 Jan. 31 (1) 71-84.

Walker, D.F., Reese J.B., & Troskie, M.I. Addressing Religions and Spiritual Issues in Trauma-Focused Cognitive Behavior Therapy for Children and Adolescents. Professional Psychology: Research and Practice (2010), vol.41, No.2, 174-180.

Watts-English, T., Fortson, B.L., Gibler, N., Hooper, S.R., & DeBellis, M.D. The Psychobiology of Maltreatment in Children. Journal of Social Issues vol. 62, No. 4, 2006, pp. 717-736.

Weiling, E., & Mittal, M. (2008). JMFT Special Section on Mass Trauma. Journal of Marital & Family Therapy. April 2008, Vol. 34, No.2, pp. 127–131.

Wethington, H.R., Hahn, R.A., Fugua-Whitely, D.S., Sipe, T.A., Crosby, A.E., Johnson, R.L., Liberman, A.M., Moscicki, E., Price, L.N., Tuma, F.K., Farris, G.K., Katra, G., & Chattopadhyay, S.K. (2008). Effectiveness of Interventions to Reduce Psychological Harm from Traumatic Events among Children and Adolescents. A Systematic Review. American Journal of Preventative Medicine.

Yeluda, R., & Flory, J.D. Differentiating Biological Correlates Risk, PTSD & Resilence Following Trauma. Journal of Traumatic Stress, Vol. 20, No.4. August 2007 pp. 435-447.

Young, R. Trauma, Attempted Suicide, and Morning Cortisol in a Community Sample of Adolescents. Journal of Traumatic Stress, Vol. 23, No.2, April 2010, pp. 288-291.

Glossary

Children: ages 0–11 years old.

Adolescents: ages 12 to 21 years old.

Bio-psychosocial: anatomical, physiological and emotional make-up of individuals that can be impacted. In this instance it refers specifically to children and adolescents.

Trauma: an emotional shock that can produce a lasting effect on a child or adolescent.

Disorders: ailments that occur due to the impact of trauma.

Assessment: the use of clinical interviews and neuropsychological instruments to determine levels of functioning.

EVIDENCE-BASED THERAPIES: PROVEN AND ESTABLISHED METHODS OF TREATMENTS FOR PARTICULAR DISORDERS.

ABOUT THE AUTHOR

Dr. Jean Johnson is a teacher, lecturer, course writer, coordinator and psychotherapist who works within the Jamaican education system. She works at both the secondary and tertiary levels. Her work engagements include project work for the Ministry of Education as well as other agencies.

www.ingramcontent.com/pod-product-compliance
Lightning Source LLC
Chambersburg PA
CBHW082147290526
45794CB00008B/3199